"...e a robot that goes to school ...es everything while you stay ...Then when school is over, it ...ngs it learned into your brain."
Daniel

"My favorite change will be when the ocean washes away California, which will leave Las Vegas with an ocean."
Michael

"...sticated series of tournaments that appeal to the most renowned gamblers."
Karina

"The sodas will make you smarter and stronger, and bacon is good for your heart."
James

"There will even be DNA locks to unlock your hotel room door. Inside your hotel room, there will be robot maids to make your bed and do your laundry."
Trevor

"Poverty is a thing of the past. Mayor Goodman 2.0 says, 'Nevada will be a happy, rich, clean place to live.'"
Anthony

"The town will have a lot more people and be really congested, so there will be streets on top of streets."
Cass

"...in a big dome ...e whole city, ...e change the ...d get rid of ...g."
...a

"Famous scientists will make a collar that can fit any animal. The collar has a big knob on it that you can spin, and then the animal can speak human languages."
Jesse

"Instead of picking up a car after you won it, a little tiny vehicle will pop out from where coins usually come out, and behind it a key ring with keys and a pad with a button on it. Push the little button and the car grows to its regular size – a brand new car!"
Tara

"I think that elementary and middle school will be combined and there will be only three grades in high school, and you can graduate when your teacher thinks it's necessary."
Kenyada

"Las Vegas will become the capital of the United States, since it will become the center of attention for the world; the President will even want to move the White House to Las Vegas."
Jose

Springs in the Desert

A Kid's History of Las Vegas

By Jonathan Peters, Ph.D.

Stephens Press • Las Vegas, Nevada

Springs in the Desert

A Kid's History of Las Vegas

Publisher: Carolyn Hayes Uber
Author: Jonathan Peters, Ph.D.
Editor: Michael Green, Ph.D.
Copy Editor: Michael Doyle, M.Ed.
Photo Editor: Joan Burkhart Whitely
Art Director: Sue Campbell
Cover Illustrator: Laura Marshall
Production Designer: Rini Twait
Publishing Coordinator: Stacey Fott

Cataloging in Publication

Peters, Jonathan.
Springs in the desert : a kid's history of Las Vegas / by
Jonathan Peters.
208 p. : ill. ; 22.9 cm.
Includes glossary.
Includes bibliographical references.
Presents a history of Las Vegas and the surrounding area
including the first Native American visitors, the ranchers, city
founders, military, Hoover Dam, and the Las Vegas strip.

[1. Las Vegas (Nev.)-History. 2. Nevada-History.]
2007   979.3'135 dc22
ISBN-10: 1-932173-5-36
ISBN-13: 978-1-932173-53-6

STEPHENS PRESS, LLC
A Stephens Media Group Company

Post Office Box 1600
Las Vegas, NV 89125-1600
www.stephenspress.com

www.kidshistoryoflasvegas.com

Printed in Hong Kong

Acknowledgements

Sponsors:
The Commission for the Las Vegas Centennial
Mountain's Edge Master Planned Community
Nevada Power
Providence Master Planned Community
Jim and Beverly Rogers

Supporting Organizations:
The Commission for the Las Vegas Centennial
Clark County School District
Communities in Schools of Southern Nevada
Junior League of Las Vegas
KVBC Channel 3
Las Vegas Review-Journal Newspapers in Education
The Nevada Community Foundation
Preferred Public Relations
Stephens Press, LLC

Las Vegas Children's History Foundation Board Members:
Julie Doyle • Stan Fuke • Sara Gardner • Louise Helton • Eileen Horn
Jeff Kutash • Bill Marion • Erica Mayer • Sheila Moulton • Libby Parker
Judy Reich • Carolyn Uber • Senator Valerie Weiner • Carolyn Wheeler

Contents

Lost Frontier Village Los Vegas

FRONTIER
MUSEUM & SALOON

77   7/3/52

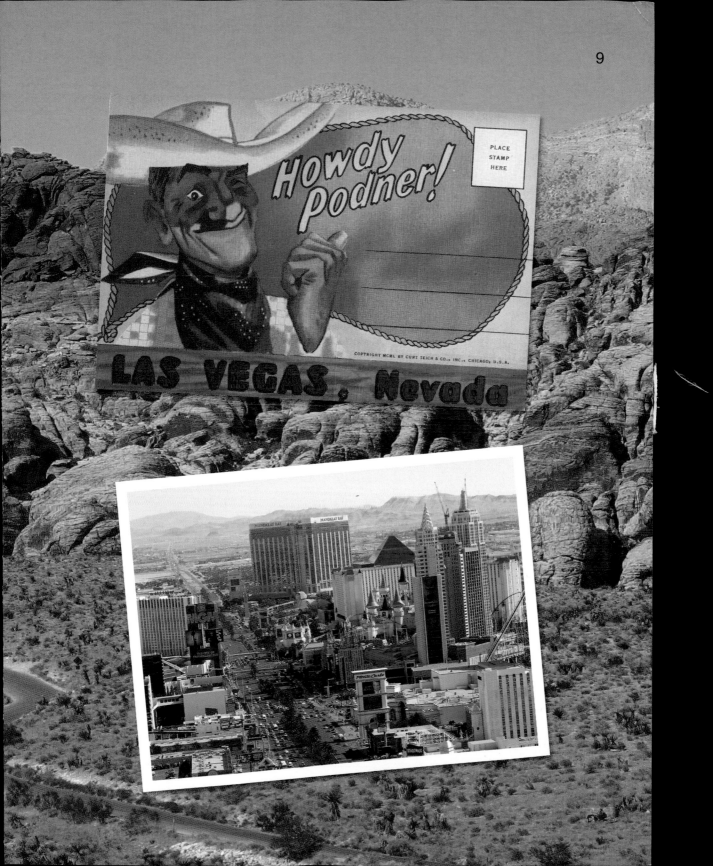

CHAPTER 1

- **First Las Vegas Visitors**

- **The Anasazi Build a City**

- **The Paiutes Camp at the Las Vegas Springs**

First Las Vegas Visitors

The first people to visit the Las Vegas Valley saw a very different place than we see today. Ten thousand years ago, water flowed in rivers through the Las Vegas Valley, lush grasses and bushes covered the land, and herds of animals roamed the valley.

The first visitors arrived in hunting parties. They were attracted by such animals as deer, elk, antelope, and mountain sheep. However, other, much larger animals also roamed the Las Vegas Valley, including wooly mammoth, mastodons, a type of camel, and even ground sloths. Early humans also had to watch out for ferocious lions and saber-toothed tigers.

The first people in Southern Nevada were called **Paleo-Indians**. This name literally means "ancient Indians." They didn't live in one place like we do;

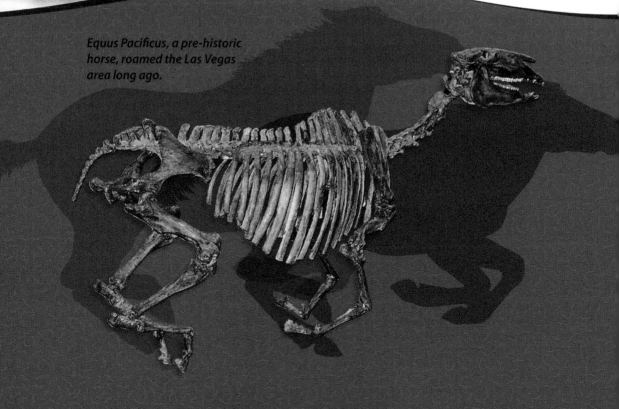

Equus Pacificus, a pre-historic horse, roamed the Las Vegas area long ago.

instead, they camped in different places, following the animals they hunted.

Paleo-Indians often set up camp in caves. That is where we find their fire circles and the tools they left behind. These tools were made out of animal bones and mastodon tusks. Since they didn't have bows and arrows, the Paleo-Indians hunted with spears. While it is rare to find a spearhead in the Nevada wilderness, it is still possible to find the chips that fell away, when they were making spearheads in their camps.

Finding Evidence of Early Humans

In 1930, archeologists discovered the remains of a prehistoric horse, a camel, and a ground sloth in Gypsum Cave. The cave is in mountains only 13 miles east of Las Vegas.

But they were most excited when they found a fire circle with ancient tools under several feet of sloth manure.

This meant people lived in the cave before the extinct sloth moved in. Carbon dating later showed that the tools and fire ring were about 10,000 years old.

The Paleo-Indians left behind pictures that we still can see today. All around Las Vegas, these ancient people carved pictures called **petroglyphs** into the rocks. These carvings may be pictures of events like big hunts. Some people say the pictures were part of Indian ceremonies. They may even be the carvings of bored children.

It's important to protect ancient petroglyphs! Don't deface rocks with graffiti. Once our ancient treasures are destroyed, they are gone forever.

Anasazi pit homes were built in a pit up to six feet deep, with standing willow branches, and parts of yucca plants woven to form the walls and roof.

The Anasazi Build a City

Almost 2,000 years ago, the **Anasazi** moved into Southern Nevada from New Mexico and Arizona. By then, it was drier and hotter in the Las Vegas Valley; therefore, the Anasazi lived along the Muddy River and the Virgin River near what are now Moapa and Overton. They planted beans, squash, and corn, damming the rivers to provide water for these crops.

The Anasazi made beautiful baskets and pots. They were also Nevada's first miners. They mined salt and turquoise. They used the salt to keep their meat from spoiling and made jewelry out of the turquoise.

Originally, the Anasazi built pit homes. They would dig holes up to six feet deep in the riverbanks. Over these holes they built a type of hut using willow branches and the stringy part of yucca plants.

The remains of this type of pit dwelling were discovered near where downtown Las Vegas is today. The pit house measured 12 feet across and was dug a foot into the ground. There was a fire ring in the middle of the hut and **metates**, or grinding stones, were found nearby. Archeologists also found a mat nearby that was made from wild grasses.

The Anasazi used the metate and mano to grind corn for flour. They made beautiful pottery that was used for food storage. Their pottery was often decorated with black and white patterns.

Later, the Anasazi built more stable homes using **adobe**, which is a combination of clay and straw. The Anasazi built homes that, like modern apartments, had several rooms under one roof. The largest of these houses had nearly 100 rooms.

Today we call the Anasazi community near the town of Overton, the Lost City or the "Pueblo Grande de Nevada." **Lake Mead** now covers the city, but it once was a community of 10,000 to 20,000 people. It

Layers of Ash Lost City

Discovering the Lost City

Mark Harrington discovered the Lost City in 1924.

While walking along the Muddy River, he found a piece of pottery that should not have been in Nevada. The pattern on the pottery piece looked like it came from the ancient Anasazi, who lived in New Mexico or Arizona.

Harrington began digging and studying the area and eventually found 77 ancient homes.

When Hoover Dam was built, Lake Mead covered the Lost City, but some of the artifacts were saved.

stretched four or five miles and was a mile wide.

Mysteriously, all of the Anasazi disappeared around 1150 A.D., not just from Nevada, but also from New Mexico and Arizona. No one knows for sure what happened to them or where they went. They simply disappeared.

What they left behind was Nevada's first ghost town. While the site of the Anasazi town now lies beneath Lake Mead, you can see some of the artifacts at the Lost City Museum in Overton, Nevada.

A view of Lake Mead, today. The site of the Lost City is underwater now.

The Paiutes Camp at the Las Vegas Springs

The **Paiute** were the people living around the Las Vegas Valley when Europeans first began exploring the Southwest. The Las Vegas Valley made a good home base for the Paiutes. They had plenty of water, shelter, and food. The Paiutes mostly hunted small animals like rabbits, squirrels, gophers, and even mice and rats. They also ate lizards and snakes, bird eggs, and even caterpillars and grasshoppers.

With food like this, it is understandable that the Paiutes ate a lot of vegetables such as squash, pumpkins, muskmelons, sunflowers, and beans. They also picked pinenuts in the mountains and mesquite beans along the Las Vegas Wash.

Ancient Chewing Gum

The Paiutes had their own gum. By roasting the stalks of the Agave plant, they made a sweet, chewy material that could be chewed just like gum.

The Paiutes lived in brush shelters called **wickiups**. Because they needed shade and protection from the wind, in the summertime they built homes made of willow branches, grass, and sagebrush. For their winter homes, the Paiutes set willow poles in a circle and tied them at the top. Then they covered the sides of the shelter with mats made of cattail plants, tree bark, and grass.

Because of the summer heat, the Paiutes wore few or no clothes except basket hats. In the winter, they wore rabbit skin blankets. They did, however, tattoo their faces and pierce their ears. In fact, they believed they could not pass into the afterlife unless their ears were pierced.

The Paiutes had everything they wanted in the Las Vegas Valley and the surrounding mountains. Soon, however, explorers and settlers would make their lives more difficult.

Remains of a brush shelter typical of the Southern Paiute people. Below are baskets made by the Washoe tribe, cousins of the Paiute.

CHAPTER 2

- **Explorers Discover the Las Vegas Valley**

- **Armijo Looks for a Shortcut**

- **Fremont Becomes the First American Visitor**

This statue of Rafael Rivera stands at Stewart Avenue just west of Mohave Road in Las Vegas.

Explorers Discover the Las Vegas Valley

Many people forget that Las Vegas was once part of Spain. Then, when Mexico won its independence, Nevada became part of Mexico. In fact, most of the Southwest United States was part of Mexico until the United States won the Mexican-American war in 1848.

The Spanish created what was known as the **Old Spanish Trail** that connected Santa Fe with Los Angeles. There were actually several different routes of this trail, but the one closest to Las Vegas followed the Virgin River south to the Colorado River, passing Las Vegas only a few miles to the east. However, no one strayed from this route to explore the Las Vegas Valley, at least not until 1829, when **Antonio Armijo** began looking for a shortcut to California.

EARLY EXPLORATIONS & THE SPANISH TRAIL 1776 - 1848

UTAH

NEVADA

to Santa fe

Littlefield

Mesquite

Spring Mountains

Snow Mountain

Sheep Range

Muddy River

Moapa Valley

(Jornada de Muerto)

Virgin River

Las Vegas Springs

Cottonwood Spring

Las Vegas Wash

Sunrise Mt.

Armijo 1829 (probable route)

O Potosi Spring

Stump Spring

Potosi Ledge

TRAIL

CALIFORNIA

Death Valley

Resting Spring

Amargosa River

COLORADO RIVER

Jedediah Smith

GRAND CA

ARIZONA

SPANISH

Mojave River

Jedediah Smith 1826

Mojave Villages

Francisco Garces 1776

Armijo Looks for a Shortcut

Instead of following the Old Spanish Trail all the way south along the Virgin and Colorado rivers, Antonio Armijo wanted to find a shortcut that would save time by cutting across the desert and mountains. Such a shortcut would take days off their journey if only enough water could be found.

On Christmas Day, Armijo set up camp on the Virgin River and sent out scouts to find a shortcut to California. All of the men returned to the camp on December 31, 1829, except for one person — a teenager named **Rafael Rivera**.

For two weeks, Rivera wandered along the Colorado River until he came to Black Canyon (where Hoover Dam is today). At this point, he left the Colorado River and traveled up the Las Vegas Wash until he found a hill he could climb and look for the rest of his party. Instead, he saw the Las Vegas Springs and the surrounding meadows. He was the first non-Indian to visit the Las Vegas Valley.

Finally, on January 7, 1830, Rivera caught up with Armijo. When Rivera told Armijo about the beautiful springs and meadows, Armijo wanted to see the springs for himself. From there, Armijo found a way over the mountains to the west. That was his shortcut to California.

Other Spanish explorers took Armijo's shortcut to California. They began calling the valley with the beautiful springs "the Meadows" or, in Spanish, Las Vegas.

Fremont becomes the First American Visitor

Most people who traveled the Old Spanish Trail were carrying supplies and items for sale to and from Los Angeles, but **John C. Fremont** had a different mission – conquest. While Mexico claimed the lands of the Southwest in the 1840s, it did not have enough people to settle the area. This meant that most of the Southwest was left largely unprotected from people like Fremont, who wanted more land for the United States.

Fremont cut across the top of Nevada to California, and then headed south. Unfortunately, when he reached the Mohave Desert, he and his men were getting low on water. The cattle pulling their wagons were weak from the lack of water and grass. Fremont stopped to kill three of the weaker cows for food. They then dried the meat to preserve it.

As they worked, a Mexican man and an eleven-year-old boy approached the camp. The man told Fremont that he and the boy were with a group of herders the Indians had attacked. Only the man and the boy escaped. The man led Fremont back to the spot of the attack, near where the town of Tecopa is today, on the California/Nevada border west of Pahrump, Nevada.

As they approached the spot of the attack, the boy's dog barked and ran to meet them. The dog had been watching over the bodies of the two dead men. The boy began crying as the dog jumped into his arms. The boy's father lay dead on the ground, but his mother was nowhere to be found.

A portrait of John C. Fremont.

After they had a small funeral and buried the bodies, the Mexican man guided Fremont and his group along the route that Antonio Armijo discovered years earlier. They traveled through Pahrump and Mountain Springs Pass. Then they went down the valley where Blue Diamond is now, past Red Rocks and finally arrived at the Las Vegas Springs.

Fremont wrote about two springs that were four or five feet deep in a valley called Las Vegas. His men ran to the springs, but found the water too warm to

Big Springs, Las Vegas

be refreshing. However, Fremont said they were great for bathing, especially since it had been some time since anyone had taken a bath.

Fremont kept a journal and drew careful maps. When he completed his exploration, he put his journal and maps in a book. The book became so popular that over 20,000 people bought it. The map and Fremont's description brought many people to Las Vegas looking for water and a place to rest on their journey to California.

CHAPTER 3

- **Settlers Move to the Las Vegas Valley**

- **Building a Fort**

- **The Lead Mine at Mount Potosi**

Settlers Move to the Las Vegas Valley

When settlers began moving west, Salt Lake City was the last city before the wild frontier. The people living in Salt Lake City didn't have enough food, livestock, or other supplies for the pioneers. The people of Salt Lake City began going to California to get supplies and food for these settlers.

Because the trip to Los Angeles was dangerous and difficult, the leaders of the **Mormon Church** decided to build a fort about halfway between Salt Lake City and Los Angeles, at the Las Vegas Springs. This fort would provide protection for travelers, water, food, and other supplies.

A group of 30 men left Salt Lake City and headed toward the Las Vegas Springs. Usually people traveled through the Nevada deserts in the winter, when it wasn't too hot. But the Mormon settlers left Salt Lake City on May 10, 1855. It took them over a month to reach the Muddy River near Moapa. By then, it was almost the hottest time of the year.

From the Muddy River to the Las Vegas Springs, there was a 55-mile stretch of desert that had no water. This stretch of the Old Spanish Trail was so difficult and dangerous that many people didn't make it. Cargo and the bones of dead mules and oxen littered the path. In fact, Mexican travelers called this section of the Old Spanish Trail the **"Journada de Muerta"** or Journey of Death.

To make this last part of the journey, the Mormon settlers split their party in half. Fifteen men left at sunset and traveled through the night and the next day without stopping. By the time they reached Las Vegas, their water was gone and they were very tired.

But the men had no time to rest. They quickly dropped the cargo from their wagons and refilled all their buckets with water. Then they returned along the path to meet the rest of the group halfway and gave them enough water to complete their journey.

After such a difficult journey, the settlers were relieved to reach Las Vegas. However, they took only one day off to rest from their long journey. The next day they began building their new fort, which would become known as the **Mormon Fort**. You can see part of this fort at the intersection of Las Vegas Boulevard and Washington Avenue.

The site of the future fort, with Frenchman's Mountain in the background.

Building a Fort

When the Mormon settlers first arrived at the Las Vegas Springs, a large camp of Paiutes already lived there. Since they didn't know how friendly the Paiutes would be, the Mormon settlers moved about four miles northeast to a hill they hoped would give them more protection.

The men set to work building a fort under the hot summer sun. Even though it was hot and they didn't have air conditioning, the men wore heavy wool clothes with long sleeves and tight-fitting collars. Their heavy beards and dark hats made them even hotter.

To get the wood they needed for the fort, the men had to go up into the mountains, where they cut down trees with axes. Then they had to hook the logs up to oxen and mules and drag the logs twenty miles back to the fort.

The fort was 150 feet wide and 150 feet long. They built it upon a foundation of stone. It had adobe walls that stood fourteen feet high. The walls were two-feet thick at the bottom and one-foot thick at the top. Peepholes were placed in the wall so the men could look through the walls if trouble arrived. They built houses inside the fort walls.

Peepholes were built in the wall of the Mormon Fort so that men could watch for signs of danger.

The old Mormon Fort today, at Las Vegas Boulevard and Washington Avenue.

As they built the fort, the settlers also dug irrigation ditches and began planting fruit trees, vegetables, grain, and cotton. They built corrals to keep cows and other animals from wandering away.

At the time, nearly 2,000 Paiutes lived around the fort. They helped the settlers by herding the livestock and watering the crops. They also helped make adobe for the fort walls. The Mormons usually paid the Paiutes with squash for their work.

At first, the crops grew well. However, drought caused many of the crops to fail. By the fall, the settlers needed 4,000 or 5,000 pounds of flour for the winter. Many of the men traveled to California to find work and buy more flour.

Desert squash such as these were used as food by the Paiutes.

The same drought that ruined the settlers' crops also wiped out the Paiute's supply of wild foods. Since the Paiutes were used to sharing, they took the settlers' food. The settlers saw this as stealing and protected their food from the hungry Paiutes. Tensions between the settlers and Paiutes arose, making it more difficult for the Mormon settlers living in the Las Vegas Valley.

The Lead Mine at Mount Potosi

Bullets were hard to come by in the Old West. First, lead had to be mined out of the mountains. Then the **ore** had to be refined to separate the lead from the rocks around it by heating the lead until the metal became liquid. Finally, the liquid lead had to be poured into bullet molds and left to cool and harden.

While making bullets was a long and expensive process, there was also a huge demand for bullets in the Old West. Settlers passing through Salt Lake City wanted to buy lots of bullets before they moved further west and faced unfriendly Indians. The settlers also needed bullets for hunting. Without bullets, they would starve.

When lead was found in Mount Potosi near Las Vegas, Mormon leaders in Salt Lake City sent miners to the new settlement at Las Vegas. When the miners arrived, they set to work breaking up the rock with pickaxes.

Hand tools for making bullets.

The Potosi mine entrance is perched upon the cliff edge 150 feet below the Summit of Mount Potosi.

At right, a prospector with his burros and gear visiting early Las Vegas.

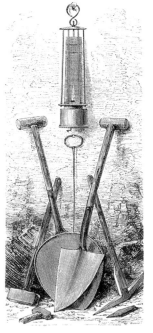

The mine was located high on the steep mountainside. The raw ore from the mountain had to be hauled down to where it could be refined. Instead of risking the lives of the mules, the miners hired Paiutes to pack thousands of pounds of rock down the mountain. They agreed to pay the Paiutes ten shirts and some food for every 10,000 pounds of ore they carried. However, after one trip down the mountain, the Paiutes walked away from the job.

The refining process required large amounts of wood to make the fires hot enough to melt the lead. Roads had to be built to the Spring Mountains, where miners cut down trees and dragged them back to the refining area. This was hard work at any time, but especially during the summer. The heat was even worse near the fires used to refine the lead.

The miners became discouraged when they discovered that the lead was not pure enough to make good bullets. The bullets they made flaked and fell apart.

A hoist and ore bucket brought minerals out of the mine. A pick and miner's light were used in the mines.

When winter came and they began running out of food, most of the miners returned to Utah. Those who stayed behind faced even more troubles with low food supplies and raiding Indians. The final blow came the next fall when the Paiutes stole the whole harvest. The Mormon settlers knew they couldn't survive the winter, so they abandoned the fort in 1858, less than three years after it was built.

The Book of Mormon was instrumental in forming the Mormon church.

Opposite page, interior room in the Mormon Fort.

CHAPTER 4

- **Ranchers Live in the Las Vegas Valley**

- **Gass Builds a Ranch**

- **The Stewarts Move to the Las Vegas Ranch**

- **The Railroad Buys the Las Vegas Ranch**

Ranchers Live in the Las Vegas Valley

A few years after the Mormon miners gave up mining lead at Mount Potosi, other people discovered silver in the lead. That is why the lead made such poor bullets. The Mormon miners had overlooked the silver and wealth in Mount Potosi.

Miners stopped for supplies at the Las Vegas Ranch before heading for the hills and their mines.

Once word got out about the silver, hundreds of fortune seekers left the mines in California and other parts of Nevada and swarmed to Mount Potosi. All of these miners needed food and supplies. The Las Vegas Ranch became the place where miners could get what they needed.

Gass Builds a Ranch

While **Octavius Decatur "O. D." Gass** was one of many people seeking a fortune mining silver at Mount Potosi, he saw that a fortune could be made selling food and supplies to the miners.

In 1865, Gass built a house near the Las Vegas Springs using part of the old Mormon Fort. He called his ranch "Los Vegas Rancho." He changed the spelling of "Las" to "Los" so that his ranch wouldn't be confused with a town 500 miles east in New Mexico named Las Vegas.

*Mr. O. D. Gass and
Mrs. Mary Virginia Gass*

Gass set up a 640-acre ranch and rest stop. Visitors could rest at the ranch while blacksmiths repaired their equipment. Gass also placed a twenty-foot long table in his dining room so visitors could enjoy the food made by Lee, the Chinese cook at the ranch.

By the mid-1870s, Gass had bought up most of the usable land in the Las

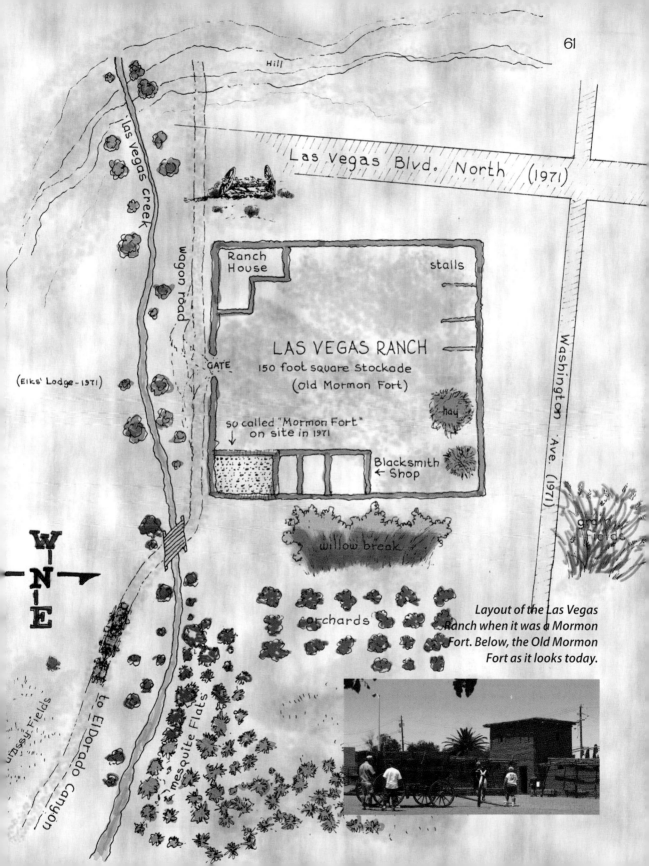

Hill

Las Vegas Blvd. North (1971)

las vegas creek

wagon road

Ranch House

stalls

LAS VEGAS RANCH
150 foot square Stockade
(Old Mormon Fort)

GATE

(Elks' Lodge - 1971)

so called "Mormon Fort" on site in 1971

hay

Blacksmith
← Shop

Washington Ave. (1971)

grain fields

willow break

W—N—S—E

orchards

Layout of the Las Vegas Ranch when it was a Mormon Fort. Below, the Old Mormon Fort as it looks today.

to ElDorado Canyon

mesquite Flats

...ssy Fields

O. D. Gass Faces Armed Warriors*

One time, a man convinced a few Paiutes that O. D. Gass owed them more beans for their labor. He took two armed warriors to visit Gass and demanded better wages.

Gass heard they were coming, so he piled all his guns on the kitchen table.

When the warriors arrived, Gass invited them inside. That was the signal for Lee, the cook, to ring the dinner bell that called the ranch-hands to dinner.

"You hear that?" Gass asked the leader. "Soon there will be men to get these guns and you won't be able to get anywhere."

At that moment, Gass' wife walked

Vegas Valley. He watered this land by digging ditches that took water from the streams and to the fields. He raised fruits, vegetables, and grain. The orchards had apples, apricots, peaches, and figs. He even had a vineyard.

Gass also grew Mexican pink beans, which he used to pay the Paiutes who helped him on his ranch. The Paiutes considered Gass generous for paying them with these beans.

While Gass was successful with his Las Vegas Ranch, the State of Nevada drove him out of business. At different times, the Las Vegas Valley was part of New Mexico and Arizona before finally becoming part of Nevada.

in and pulled the rifle away from one of the warriors. She then turned the man's own gun on him.

Mary Gass was well known for her shooting ability. In fact, the Indians called her "long eye" because of how well she shot a gun.

The warriors knew they were defeated. However, Gass was generous and gave them a couple of cows as a peace offering.

When the Paiutes found out what happened, they were so ashamed they made the ringleader wear a dress and work with the women as a punishment.

When Las Vegas was part of Arizona, Gass wrote the bill that created Pah-Ute County in Arizona. This county covered what is now Clark County and part of northwest Arizona. Gass became the Arizona territorial representative of this county.

In 1867, the United States Congress passed a law that allowed the State of Nevada to make Pah-Ute County part of Lincoln County in Nevada.

For a time, Gass ignored Nevada's claims. He said his ranch was still part of Arizona, and he would not pay taxes to Nevada. After two years of legal battles, the state of Nevada won and demanded two years worth of back taxes from Gass.

Gass did not have enough money to pay all these taxes, so he tried to sell his ranch. Unfortunately, no one was interested in buying it. So Gass used the ranch as **collateral** to borrow $5,000 from Archibald Stewart. Unable to pay back the money, Gass packed up his family, abandoned his Las Vegas Ranch, and moved to California in 1881.

The Stewarts Move to the Las Vegas Ranch

After O. D. Gass failed to pay off his debt and left the Las Vegas Ranch, **Archibald Stewart** became the owner of the ranch. Unfortunately, Mr. Stewart lived on the ranch only two years before he was murdered.

On that fateful day, Mr. Stewart returned home after delivering produce and livestock to miners in Eldorado Canyon. His wife, **Helen Stewart**, told him she had argued with one of his employees who had demanded more pay. When she did not give it to him, the employee quit and went to work for the nearby Kiel Ranch. This ranch was a hangout for outlaws.

These pictures show the Las Vegas Ranch at the time of the Stewarts' occupation. Mrs. Helen Stewart relaxes on the porch with her dogs; the interior of the home; and portraits of Mr. and Mrs. Stewart.

After eating lunch and resting, Mr. Stewart picked up his rifle and told his wife he was headed out to shoot a steer. Instead, he took a long route to the Kiel Ranch, located where Carey Avenue and Losee Road cross today.

When Mr. Stewart arrived at the Kiel Ranch, there was a brief gunfight. Mr. Stewart was shot in the head and died. When it was over, Conrad Kiel wrote a note and sent it to Mrs. Stewart. The note said, "Mrs Sturd send a team and take Mr. Sturd away he is dead. C. Kiel."

Even though she was pregnant with her fifth child, Helen Stewart rode to the

Spelling Kiel

Conrad Kiel only went to school for a couple years; therefore, he wasn't good at spelling. For instance, he spelled his last name Kiel, Keil, and Kyle. While his ranch was called Kiel Ranch, the canyon where he had his logging business is called Kyle Canyon.

This woman, called Paiute Annie, is wearing the traditional "basket hat" of the Southern Paiute.

Below, a Paiute man who was a worker at the Stewart Ranch, wears the western clothes his employers preferred.

Kiel Ranch, where she found the body of her husband lying on the ground, covered with a blanket. She took his body to the Las Vegas Ranch and buried him.

Back then, it was unheard of for a woman to run a ranch by herself, but that is exactly what Helen Stewart did. Shortly after burying her husband, she gave birth to her fifth child and continued to run the ranch.

At first, Mrs. Stewart wanted to sell the ranch, but she heard a rumor that the railroad would soon pass through the Las Vegas Valley. Instead of selling the ranch, she began buying more land until she owned 2,000 acres.

In 1902, Mrs. Stewart sold most of her ranch to **Senator William Clark** of Montana, so that he could use it for his railroad. The land that she did not sell she kept for her family. She also gave some land to the Paiutes. This land became the Paiute Colony on North Main Street in Las Vegas.

Mrs. Stewart was an important person in Las Vegas. She died of cancer on March 6, 1926. Her funeral was one of the largest Las Vegas has seen. People traveled from all over to pay respects to the "First Lady of Las Vegas."

Young Southern Paiute dancers join in a dance at a Pow Wow celebration.

Las Vegas Paiute Colony

The land Helen Stewart gave the Paiutes is known as the Las Vegas Colony. For a long time, the Colony had no running water or sewers. When the Paiutes asked the United States government for help, the government told them to move to the reservation in Moapa. But the Paiutes did not want to leave their home.

By selling crafts and tobacco to tourists, the Paiutes earned a humble living. In this way, they have protected their culture.

In 1983, the federal government gave the Southern Paiutes 3,840 acres of land northwest of Las Vegas. The Paiutes are developing this land today.

Currently, an eight-foot high wall surrounds the Las Vegas Colony near downtown Las Vegas. This wall protects the fewer than 40 homes in the Colony.

A grandfather walks with his little granddaughter at the Pow Wow.

The Railroad Buys the Las Vegas Ranch

Before there were airplanes, it took a long time to travel across the United States. The train offered the fastest way to travel in 1900. However, trains were limited to where there were tracks. This meant that if you lived in Las Vegas before 1905, the only way you could visit a relative in a distant city was to ride a horse or mule. Even if you were lucky enough to own a car, the roads were so bad in Southern Nevada, you had to drive slowly and would often get stuck.

If you lived in a town where the train stopped, you could visit distant cities in a matter of days. You could receive mail shortly after a person sent it to you, or get

NEVADA

UTAH

CALIFORNIA

ARIZONA

LINCOLN COUNTY
CLARK COUNTY

NYE COUNTY

Pioche

Eagle Valley

Uvada   to Salt Lake City

Caliente
(Culverwell Ranch)

Clover Valley

Delamar

Pahranagat Valley

Meadow Valley Wash

to Bullfrog, Rhyolite
and Beatty
___ miles from Las Vegas
Las Vegas & Tonopah RR

Ash Meadows
and Beatty

Pahrump Valley

Indian Springs
Ranch

Tule Springs

Kyle
Ranch

Manse
Ranch

McWilliams
Las Vegas Townsite   Las Vegas Ranch
Clark's Las Vegas
Townsite

Moapa Valley

Virgin Valley

St Thomas

Goodsprings

old
Evanpah

Tonopah & Tidewater RR

Los Angeles & Salt Lake RR

San Pedro

Crucero

Evanpah

Manvel

California E

Searchlight

Eldorado
Canyon

Colorado

Kingman

Ludlow

William Clark's Bribes

William Clark was well known for his bribes. Not only
did he bribe people to advance his businesses,
but he also used bribes to become a U.S. Senator.
William Clark defended his bribes by saying,
"I never bought a man who wasn't for sale."

William Clark waves from the back of a train car.

a newspaper that was only days old. You could also have an important tool or toy sent to you by train.

Senator William Clark was looking for a good point halfway between Los Angeles and Salt Lake City for a train stop. This train stop would be a place where the steam engines could take on more water. As long as the trains were stopping, they also could be repaired or be loaded with more ice for keeping their cargo cool.

Helen Stewart's ranch presented the perfect place for such a rail stop. It had plenty of water and lots of room for a railroad station. The only problem was there was no town of Las Vegas. The railroad company would have to build a town near the Las Vegas Springs.

This rail car served as the first train depot until the permanent building was completed in 1906.

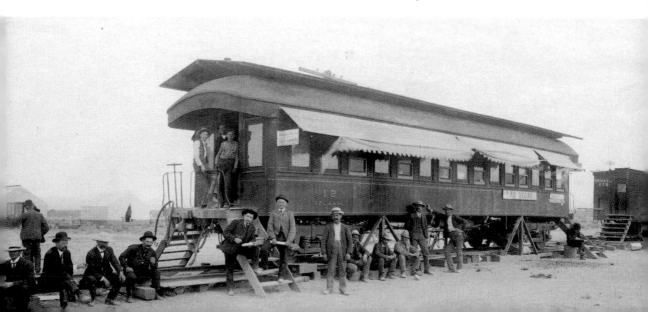

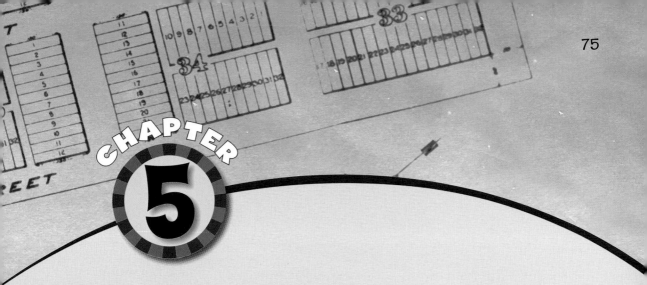

CHAPTER 5

- **The City of Las Vegas Is Born**

- **Ragtown Becomes West Las Vegas**

- **Old Town Becomes North Las Vegas**

- **Clark County is Born**

- **Water Becomes a Problem**

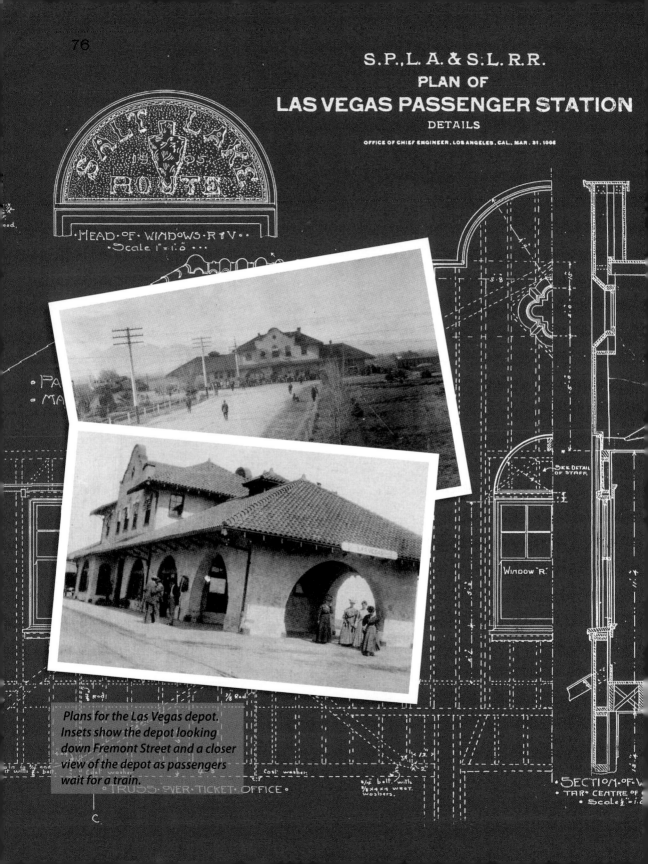

Plans for the Las Vegas depot. Insets show the depot looking down Fremont Street and a closer view of the depot as passengers wait for a train.

The City of Las Vegas Is Born

In 1905, the railroad company marked out streets and city blocks in the empty desert. The plans for the city of Las Vegas covered 110 acres from Stewart Avenue to the north, Garces Avenue to the south, Main Street to the west, and Fifth Street to the east. That whole area made up 40 square blocks.

The Plaza Hotel now stands where the old depot in the photo at left once stood.

The auctioneer at work.

On May 15, 1905, the railroad company held an **auction** to sell lots in the new town of Las Vegas. People arrived from all over to buy a part of this new town.

The weather had been cool, but on May 15, the sun rose hot over the Las Vegas Valley. While the auctioneer stood on a shaded platform, the bidders stood in the hot sun with no shade. Since the bidders viewed the auction as a special event, they had dressed in formal wool suits. Eventually it got so hot, the men removed their jackets. However, they kept their shirt collars tight at the neck and their long sleeves rolled down.

A signal light for the train crossing.

Entire families lived in temporary tent shelters. Children helped with the work.

Hotel Las Vegas

At lunchtime, people walked to the Hotel Las Vegas, hoping for shade and refreshment, but when the hotel owner opened the door, a blast of heat hit him. The temperature inside the hotel was 128 degrees.

The hotel was not like any hotel we have today. It was actually a large tent. The hotel owner didn't know about putting a "fly" or extra tarp above the tent to keep the sun's rays from shining directly on the tent. If he had used a fly, he could have kept his hotel cool and people could have found shade from the hot sun.

The floors and the bottom part of the sides of board tents were partially built with lumber.

When temperatures reached 110 degrees at 3:00 p.m., the auctioneer put an end to the auction. The auction resumed the next morning at 8:00 a.m., and by the end of the day, most of the remaining lots were auctioned off. Las Vegas was a town.

Construction of the new town began immediately. By the end of the first day, several buildings already had walls, and companies were doing business before their roofs were put up. Even the lumber from the auctioneer platform sold for $7, as people scrambled for building supplies.

In the first month, a post office was built, along with banks, warehouses, restaurants, gambling houses, saloons, and hotels. Once the businesses were in place, people began working on their houses, though most people continued to live in tents.

The chop houses of Fremont Street in the past are very different from Fremont Street today.

Early Hotels

The first Las Vegas hotels were just large tents. Only a canvas sheet separated the "rooms," which had one double bed and little else. Two people shared the bed even if they didn't know each other.

A tent with a brass bed . . . a luxury lodging.

One Las Vegas hotel owner had a unique way of keeping his beds free of **lice**.

When a man wanted a bed, the owner told him the hotel was full, even if plenty of beds were available. The owner invited the man to sit and rest near a stove until a bed opened up.

While the man waited, the owner watched him. If he scratched his head or body, the owner sent him away. However, if the man did not scratch, the owner assumed the man did not have lice and gave him a bed.

Chop houses on Fremont Street served the first "fast food" for train travelers.

The First Las Vegas School

In 1905, the people of Las Vegas rushed to get a school ready for the fall. They raised enough money to change an old building into a school. But the school wasn't ready until October 2, so the students got an extra long summer vacation.

Even though the school year started late, it also ended early. The town ran out of money by March 30 and had to cancel classes for the year.

The school had fifty or sixty students when it opened in October, with only two teachers. When classes were canceled in March, there were 81 students and still only two teachers.

An early class at the Las Vegas school.

While buildings were being built in Las Vegas, the **utilities** we enjoy today were not available.

There was no electricity for the first year in Las Vegas. The townspeople started the Consolidated Power and Telephone Company (it is now called Nevada Power Company). They made an agreement with the railroad company to use an extra generator at the icehouse to power the new town.

Unfortunately, there wasn't enough electricity for everyone, so the railroad company got all of the electricity during the day and the townspeople got it in the evenings. The generator was turned off at 10 p.m. They didn't have electricity to power their fans during the heat of the day or at night when they were trying to sleep.

Girls enjoyed playing basketball. However, the uniforms were hot.

Finally, the new power company purchased another generator named "Old Betsy" that provided electricity for the town of Las Vegas all day long.

The new homes and businesses didn't have running water. People had to carry water all summer long. Finally, in September, the water company began laying water pipes in the town. These pipes were made with redwood boards tied together with wire.

Even when water did arrive at people's homes, it wasn't clean. The water company warned people to boil their water, especially since people swam in the springs and cows drank from the springs. People also complained that tadpoles and bugs were coming out of their kitchen faucets. One person said the body of a lizard came out of her faucet.

Desert Coolers

Since there was very little electricity in Las Vegas, people didn't have refrigerators to keep their food from spoiling. Instead, they built "desert coolers."

These coolers were wooden boxes wrapped in blankets. Part of this wrapping stretched upward to a metal container filled with water. Water would seep through the material and run down the blankets to the box. The water in the blanket would then **evaporate**, pulling heat out, away from the wooden box, thus keeping the contents cool.

Heavy object holds blanket in a pan of water.

Evaporation of water pulls heat out of the box.

Breeze blows through the wet cloth.

Drip pan catches run-off and keeps cloth wet.

Worse, Las Vegas had no sewer system for eight years. The townspeople passed a law that all toilets had to be enclosed in metal boxes. Unfortunately, the nearest police officer was miles away in Pioche, so no one was around to enforce the toilet law. Also, the townspeople could do nothing about trains that dumped sewage right onto the tracks. Back then, the toilets on the train were nothing more than holes in the floor of the train car.

Besides the smell of all this waste in the summer heat, the flies breeding in the waste made life miserable. The wild burros wandering through town, eating trash along the streets, also attracted flies. Back then, few tents and houses had screens like we have on our windows today. And since they had no air-conditioning, the only way to cool the house was to keep all of the windows and doors open. This meant people could not sleep at night with all the flies buzzing around. Things were so bad that many people left Las Vegas before the first hot summer was over.

Ragtown Becomes West Las Vegas

When William Clark started the town of Las Vegas on May 15, 1905, there was already a town in the Las Vegas Valley. Not only did Clark ignore this other town, but he also worked very hard to put it out of business.

Before Helen Stewart sold her Las Vegas Ranch to Clark for his railroad and town, she hired a man named **J. T. McWilliams** to **survey** her ranch. McWilliams carefully did his job, but he saw an opportunity. He knew the railroad company would focus on laying train tracks across the desert before building the town. That gave him enough time to buy property near the Las Vegas Springs and the road to the gold mining towns of Rhyolite and Bullfrog. Today this road is Highway 95 and McWilliams' town was located just north of where the Spaghetti Bowl is presently.

I-95's Spaghetti Bowl, which is just south of where Ragtown once was.

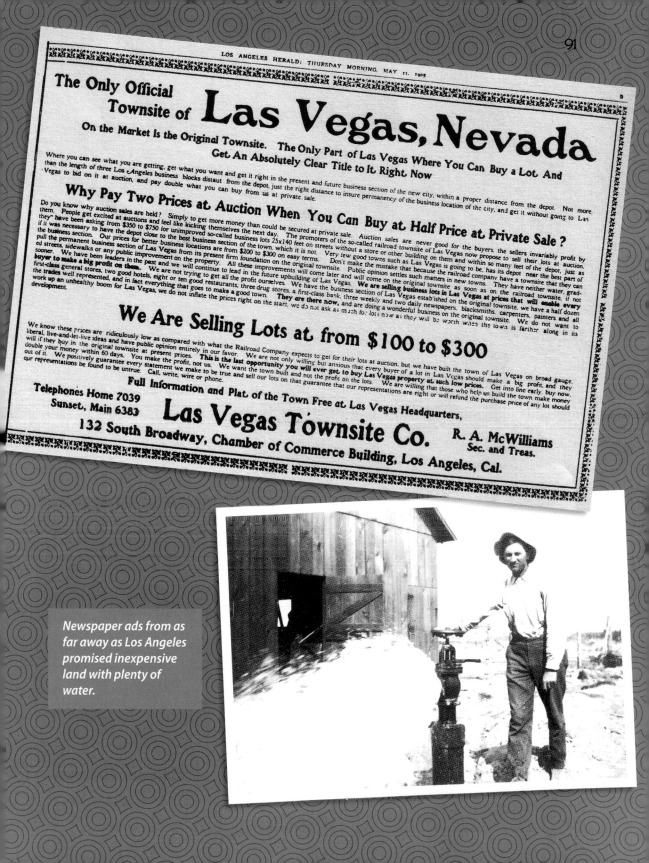

Newspaper ads from as far away as Los Angeles promised inexpensive land with plenty of water.

McWilliams began selling lots in his town in 1904, a year before Clark held his auction. McWilliams' town quickly grew to 1,500 people. The first people to buy lots were miners, cowboys, gamblers, and even a few thieves. The cheap land also attracted immigrants. Soon Mexican, Chinese, Italian, Finnish, Australian, Irish, Greek, and Spanish people lived in the small town.

Scenes from Ragtown.

The new town had a hotel, store, and four restaurants. It also had ten bars and gambling halls. These businesses were not in buildings like those we have today. They were in large tents that were always in danger of being blown over or catching fire. Since few wood or brick buildings were in McWilliams' town, people began to call it "**Ragtown**."

The icehouse incident

J. T. McWilliams thought he was going to get his revenge on William Clark. When the railroad company laid the train tracks through the Las Vegas Valley, they were slightly off. They laid tracks across McWilliams' land. McWilliams didn't say anything at the time, even though he knew about the mistake.

Then, there were no refrigerators, much less refrigerated boxcars. The only way to keep produce and meat from rotting was to pack them in ice. If all the ice melted and the food spoiled, the railroad company would lose a lot of money. Therefore, the icehouse was very important to the railroad company.

When Clark was looking for a place to build the icehouse, he found a nice piece of land on his side of the railroad tracks across from McWilliams' land. He put people to work building the icehouse, which was supposed to be the largest building in Las Vegas.

McWilliams saw immediately that the icehouse was actually being built on his property. Instead of letting Clark know, he waited until the foundation was laid, and they were beginning to work on the walls. He then went to Clark and offered to sell him the land under the icehouse for $1,000.

Instead of paying McWilliams, Clark stopped the construction. He abandoned the half-finished building and began building a new icehouse on his own property.

ICE
Drinks

Clark tried to shut down Ragtown by cutting off the water to the town. When Clark bought Mrs. Stewart's ranch, he also bought all the water rights to the Las Vegas Springs, which meant that all water coming from the springs belonged to him. He controlled who got the water and how much they got.

Fortunately for McWilliams, so much water was underground in the Las Vegas Valley, all the townspeople needed to do was dig several feet into the ground and fresh water would come bubbling to the surface. Unfortunately for us today, the people living in Ragtown didn't bother to "cap" their wells. Instead, they let the wells flow out onto the ground all day long, every day, wasting all that water.

The second ice house.

At the bottom of the page, the ice wagon makes deliveries.

Looking down Bonanza Road toward the former West Las Vegas site.

However, the wells weren't enough to keep people in Ragtown. The day after Clark's auction, many people in Ragtown packed up their tents and moved across the track to the new town of Las Vegas. Even the bank, which was a wood building, moved to Las Vegas. The owner put the bank on large boards and towed it a couple miles to Fremont Street.

Ragtown would always struggle, even after it became known as West Las Vegas. It was the place where poor people and

A West Las Vegas neighborhood, before being bulldozed for I-15.

people of color were sent to live. CIty officials refused to improve West Las Vegas; instead, they let the town fall apart.

In the 1960s, when the new paved freeway (I-15) came to Las Vegas, city officials decided to put it through West Las Vegas. They bulldozed hundreds of homes to make way for the road and left all those people without homes. Even today, this area is a poor neighborhood. It appears William Clark won the war between Las Vegas and Ragtown.

Tom Williams, the founder of North Las Vegas.

Old Town Becomes North Las Vegas

As small as Las Vegas was in 1917, it was too big for some people. When **Tom Williams** visited Las Vegas in 1917, he thought it would be a great place for farming with all of the water and empty land. However, he thought the city of Las Vegas was a dusty, smelly town. So he purchased 160 acres a mile north of town. Two years later, Williams realized he could make more money selling his land than farming it. He set aside 100 acres to create his own town. He dug a well, put in roads and brought in power lines. Then he began selling lots. For some reason, this new town became known as "Old Town." Today we call it North Las Vegas.

Williams did not believe government was a good thing. He thought regulations, rules, and police officers kept people from becoming the best they could be and doing what they wanted. So, when Williams built his town, he offered churches free land. He believed church people would be better at running the town than a government. Unfortunately, church people were not attracted to a town without police officers.

Below, Tom Willams (center), his wife, and a friend with his dog.

In 1919, the 18th Amendment of the United States Constitution outlawed alcohol. You couldn't make, sell, or drink alcohol until the law was repealed in 1933. Since North Las Vegas had no police officers, **moonshiners**, or those who made illegal alcohol, moved to North Las Vegas to set up their businesses.

Even though Williams did not drink, he kept his word and did not enforce the new laws against alcohol. Soon, moonshiners owned almost half of the town. They built tunnels where they could hide their alcohol-making operations.

Old Town had no government for 13 years. However, when the town needed a school, residents formed a type of government. They also decided they needed a better name for their town rather than "Old Town."

Williams didn't want the town named for him, so the leaders came up with two choices: Vegas Verde ("green meadows" in Spanish) or North Las Vegas. The name North Las Vegas was chosen because two of the people who wanted the town to be named Vegas Verde were absent when the vote was taken. If they had showed up, North Las Vegas probably would now be named Vegas Verde.

One long-time Las Vegas resident said that the laundry housed a still, and the bottling company next door delivered the moonshine.

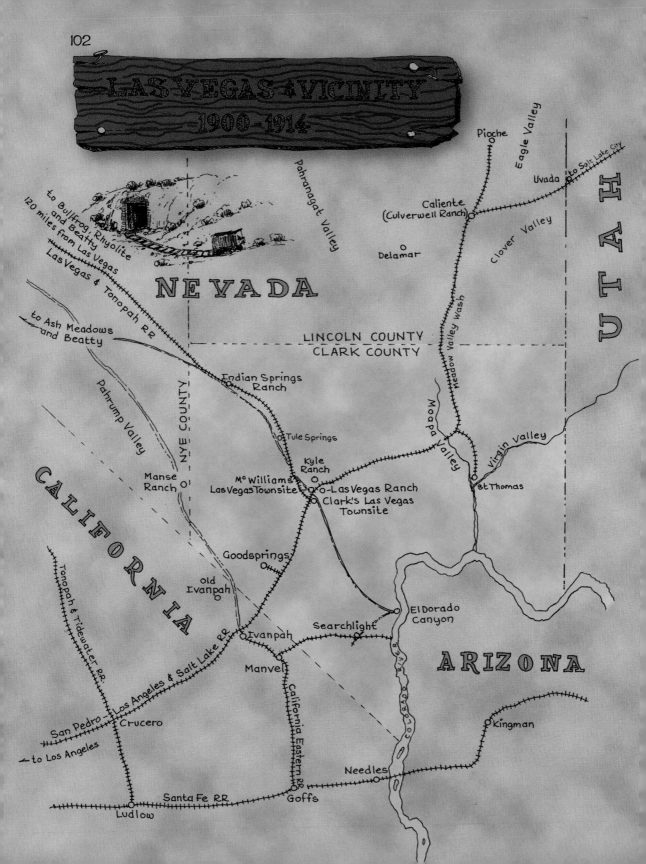

LAS VEGAS & VICINITY
1900-1914

Pioche

Eagle Valley

to Salt Lake City

Uvada

Caliente
(Culverwell Ranch)

Clover Valley

UTAH

O Delamar

Pahranagat Valley

to Bullfrog, Rhyolite
and Beatty
120 miles from Las Vegas

Las Vegas & Tonopah RR

NEVADA

to Ash Meadows
and Beatty

LINCOLN COUNTY
CLARK COUNTY

Pahrump Valley

NYE COUNTY

Indian Springs
Ranch

Meadow Valley Wash

Moapa Valley

Virgin Valley

Manse
Ranch O

Tule Springs O

Kyle
Ranch
O

St Thomas

McWilliams
Las Vegas Townsite

o-o-Las Vegas Ranch
Clark's Las Vegas
Townsite

O

Goodsprings

CALIFORNIA

old
Ivanpah

Tonopah & Tidewater R.R.

Los Angeles & Salt Lake RR

Ivanpah O

Searchlight

ElDorado
Canyon

COLORADO RIVER

ARIZONA

Manvel

California Eastern RR

San Pedro

Crucero

to Los Angeles

O Kingman

Needles

Santa Fe RR

Goffs

Ludlow

Clark County is Born

When the United States took the Southwest from Mexico, the area around Las Vegas was part of New Mexico, and then Arizona. Later, the state of Nevada claimed the area as part of Nevada. Since few people lived on this dry land, the Nevada Legislature made all of Southern Nevada part of Lincoln County.

Pioche is the **county seat** for Lincoln County. Pioche, and the mining towns around it, once had thrived. However, when the mines began running out of gold and silver, people left the towns. While those towns were suffering, the mining towns of Searchlight and Goodsprings in Southern Nevada began growing. When the railroad came to Las Vegas, it also began growing. The people in Southern Nevada didn't want to travel hundreds of miles to Pioche to take care of county business or to go to court when they were sued or in trouble with the law.

Citizens show their support for county division.

Below, a young Las Vegas girl dresses up for the festivities.

While many people in Southern Nevada favored creating a new county, they could not agree on where the county seat should be. Searchlight argued that since it was the largest town, it should be the county seat. But Las Vegas argued that since it was almost in the exact center of the new county, it should be the county seat.

In the end, Las Vegas won, and the Nevada Legislature created Clark County on July 1, 1909. The county was named for William Clark, who brought the railroad to Southern Nevada, even though he never lived in Nevada and visited it only occasionally when his railroad and Las Vegas were being built.

The depot is decorated with banners to celebrate the Fourth of July in this undated photo.

Letting wells run continuously was a common practice at one time, a factor in later water shortages.

Water Becomes a Problem

When William Clark bought Helen Stewart's ranch in 1902, he also bought the rights to all the water coming out of the Las Vegas Springs. Since he and the railroad company kept all the water for themselves and the people living in Las Vegas, people living outside of the original townsite had to dig their own wells.

Thanks to a lot of underground water, all a person needed to do was dig down six to nine feet and the water came rushing to the surface without the need for pumps. But without pumps or some sort of cap on the well, the water continued to bubble up all day, every day. Some of this water was used for watering crops, but most of it was wasted. The extra water flowed back into the ground or down the Las Vegas Wash and into the Colorado River, where it was taken to the ocean.

As more people moved to Las Vegas, they needed more water for drinking, bathing, and watering lawns. Soon, the Las Vegas Springs could not keep up with demand. Other towns noticed that their wells had less water. In a short time, the land known for all its water faced a water shortage.

Airdome PROGRAM

Week Commencing Su...

SUNDA...

...NCE TA...

...US.
...rtoon and Wee...

...SDAY
...DRICKS in "One
...e."
...EEKLY.

...DNESDAY
...ecial!! "SECRET
..." with All Star
...g Robert War-

The people of early Las Vegas found outdoor activities to help them keep cool, such as swimming at the Old Ranch, or watching movies at the Airdome in the cool of the evening.

...TO ...
...Cast.

ADMISSION: 15c and 25c.
Tax Included.

Keep The Family
COOL
All Summer

Staying Cool without Air Conditioning

Before air conditioning, people tried different things to stay cool, often wasting water in the process.

For instance, people would cover their windows with fabric. Then they would hook a garden hose to the top of the window so that the water ran down the cloth. They would then put a fan inside the window, blowing inward. This would pull cool air into the room. It would also waste all the water pouring over the fabric and draining into the ground.

Electric fans were a great help in coping with the summer heat.

Lake Mead shows the "bathtub ring" of white, revealing the toll that drought and heavy demand for water takes.

Some relief came after **Hoover Dam** was built and a large lake, called **Lake Mead**, formed behind the dam. However, water did not arrive soon enough. By the summer of 1949, Las Vegas began running out of water.

Lake Mead did eventually provide enough water to avoid a crisis and Las Vegas continued to grow. Unfortunately, years of drought with thousands of people moving to Las Vegas and millions more visiting Las Vegas every year have put a strain on the water supply.

This is why people living in Las Vegas must watch how much water they use. The good news is that despite all the people moving to Las Vegas, the amount of water each person uses has gone down. It is only through this **conservation** of water that Las Vegas will continue to be a growing and beautiful city.

Water brought people to the Las Vegas Valley in the first place. Water helps Las Vegas continue to grow. We need to remember how important water is to Las Vegas and not waste it.

All residents of Las Vegas can help to conserve water. Watch out for running hoses and leaky faucets!

The Water Cycle in the Las Vegas Valley

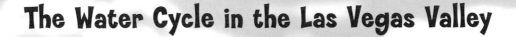

Rainfall

Rainfall

Waste Water
Treatment

Sewers and Storm Drains

Homes

Waste Water

Waste Water

Businesses

Fresh Water

Fresh Water

Fresh Water
Treatment

Water Storage
Reservoirs

Underground Aquifer

Snowfall

Evaporation

Rain run-off
and snowmelt

Lake Mead

Las Vegas Wash

Water Intake

Hoover Dam

Fresh Water Pipeline

Colorado
River

CHAPTER 6

- **Hoover Dam Saves Las Vegas**

- **Hard Economic Times**

- **Dam Construction Begins**

- **People Struggle to Survive**

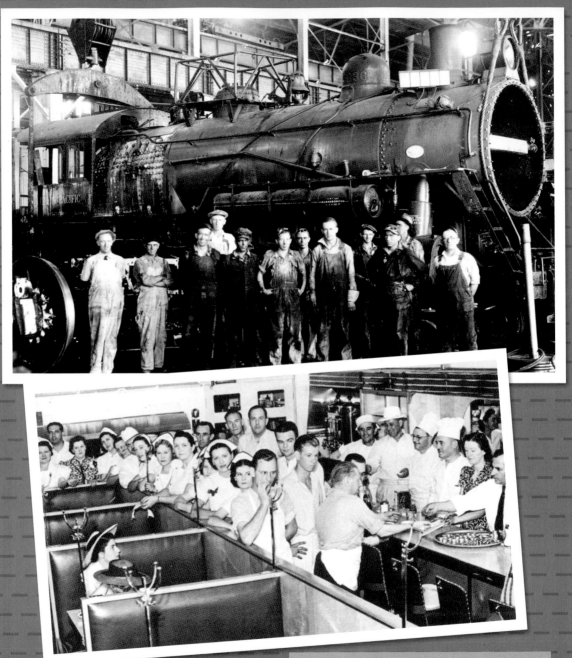

Railroad machinists pose in front of an engine in the Union Pacific's Las Vegas machine shop. Below, a Las Vegas diner's workers line up to be paid their wages in silver dollars.

Hoover Dam Saves Las Vegas

Things looked bad for Las Vegas in the 1920s. In 1922, there was a national railroad strike. Workers joined together and refused to work until their demands were heard, to protest low wages.

Hard Economic Times

However, when the workers are not working, they are not being paid. As the railroad strike went on, many families in Las Vegas began to suffer. The worst blow came after the strike ended. The railroad company decided to teach Las Vegas a lesson and moved its operations from Las Vegas to Caliente.

Since the railroad was the major business in town, many people lost their jobs when the company moved. Many of the companies in town also suffered. Soon, all of Las Vegas faced troubling times.

To make matters worse, the United States was about to enter the **Great Depression**. During the Great Depression, many banks went out of business. This meant people lost their savings, and businesses lost their funding. As businesses went **bankrupt**, people lost their jobs and had no money to save in banks. Without work or savings, people had no money for food. Many people began starving in the United States.

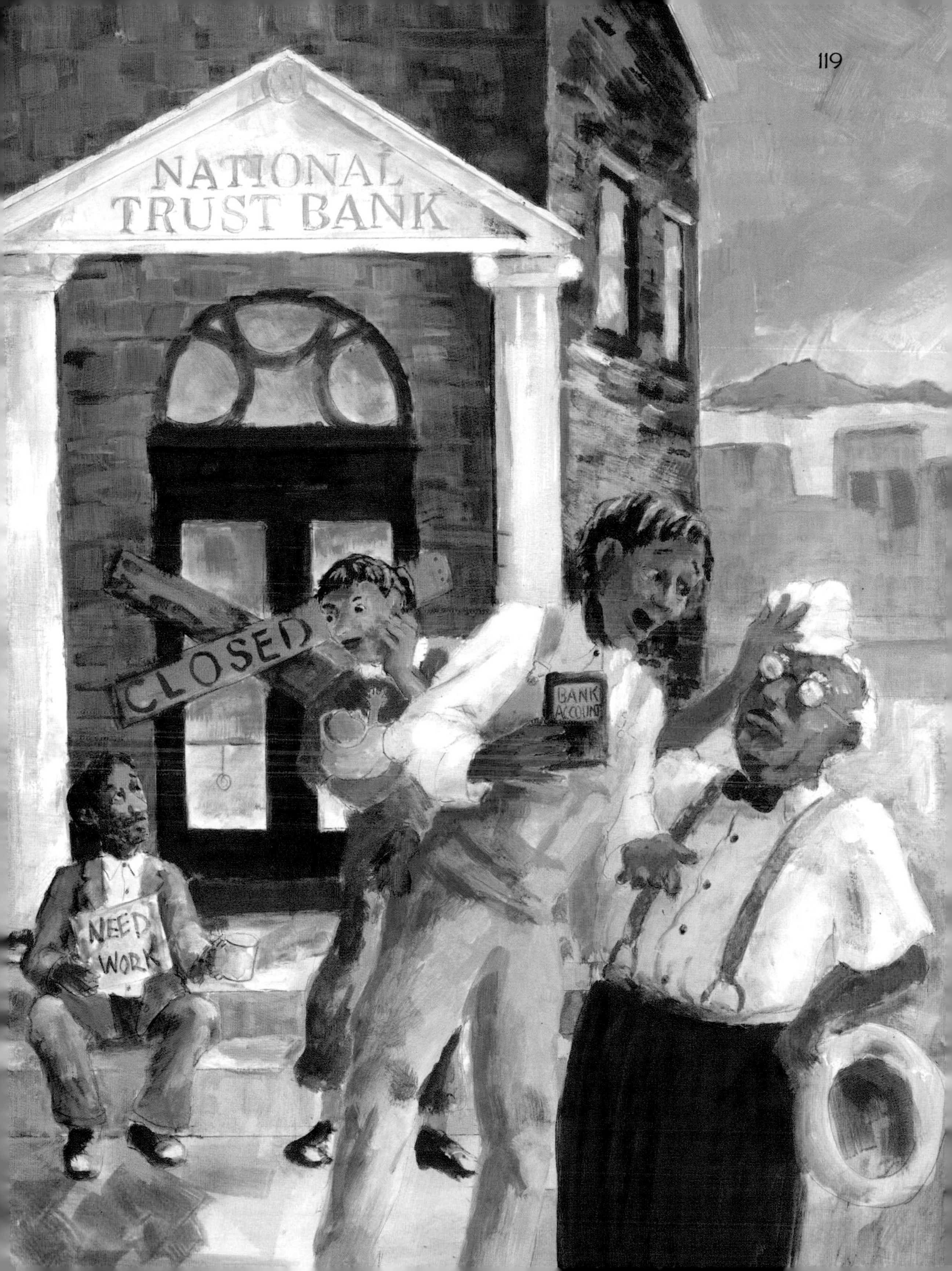
NATIONAL
TRUST BANK
CLOSED
BANK
ACCOUNT
NEED
WORK

Dam Construction Begins

The one thing that saved Las Vegas was the construction of Hoover Dam on the Colorado River.

It was the tallest dam in the world when it was built. It was 726 feet high and more than 1,200 feet long. It was so large that a highway was built on top of the dam to connect Nevada and Arizona.

A project this large required up to 5,000 hard working people at a time. The people of Las Vegas hoped all those people would live in their town while working on the dam. But the project was too large and Las Vegas was too far away. So the company in charge of dam construction built a new town closer to the dam. They called the town **Boulder City**, because at that time the dam was named Boulder Dam.

Over a span of four years, Hoover Dam took shape. The small photo at far left shows that the river has been diverted so that construction can begin. The remaining three small photos show steps in the process with the completed dam below, right.

People Struggle to Survive

Only those who worked on the dam could live in Boulder City. Everyone else waiting for a job to open up had to wait in Las Vegas. Unfortunately, during the Great Depression, a lot of people wanted to work at the dam. More than 12,000 men applied for work on the dam, but only 5,250 were hired at first. This meant a lot of disappointed people waited in Las Vegas for someone to die or move away.

At the time, only about 5,000 people lived in Las Vegas. The town was not ready for the 12,000 men and their families coming to Las Vegas to look for work. There was not enough food in the town to feed the starving families, or enough houses and beds to shelter the people. Many people had to sleep outside and search for food.

Top, workers were transported to the dam site on "Bertha," a large bus. Middle, other vehicles for worker transport. Bottom, for some, cottages were provided. However, as time went on, funds for this type of housing dwindled.

Thousands of people came looking for work, but there were not enough jobs for all. Many families camped out in the desert hoping for a chance to work on the dam. There were not even enough cottages for all the hired workers and their families. These people lived in tents also.

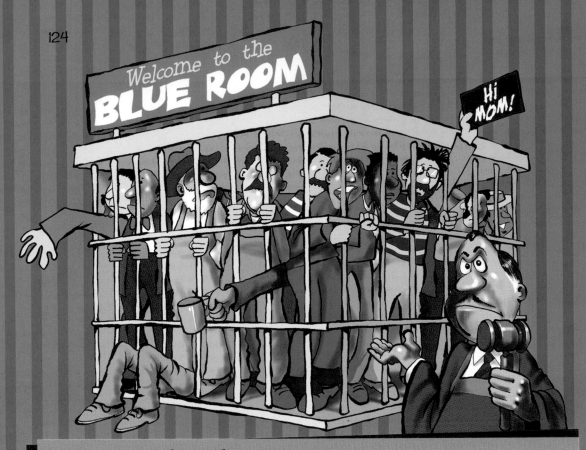

Hobos in the Blue Room

People who were looking for work, but without a place to live were called "hobos."

To keep hobos out of Las Vegas, city officials passed laws to outlaw begging and sleeping in the streets.

The judge would tell the policemen to round up all the hobos they could find and bring them to the court. The judge then explained that if the hobos were not out of town by sunrise, they would spend 10 days in the "Blue Room."

The Blue Room was the name for the Las Vegas jail. It was a single room designed for 10 or 12 people. On some weekends, though, 150 men were crammed into it. There was no air conditioning. Worse, there was no plumbing in the building.

One night in the Blue Room was usually enough to get the hobos to move out of town. Usually they moved to Old Town (North Las Vegas), where there were no policemen or jails.

On the plus side, the dam project did bring a lot of business to Las Vegas. Most of the supplies to build the dam came through Las Vegas, either by the railroad or by truck. Other things they needed for workers at the dam such as milk, fresh vegetables, and bread, also came from Las Vegas.

Most important for Las Vegas' future were tourists beginning to come to Las Vegas to see the amazing dam. These tourists stayed in hotels and ate in restaurants in Las Vegas. Even after the dam was completed in 1935, thousands of people from all over the country stayed in Las Vegas while they toured the dam or enjoyed Lake Mead.

Below, President Franklin D. Roosevelt speaks at the dedication of the new Boulder Dam. The name of the dam was later changed to Hoover Dam. Bottom, Fremont Street decorated for Helldorado Days in the 1930s. The arch boasts Las Vegas' connection with the dam.

BLACK CANYON DAMSI
COLORADO RIVER

Left, the Colorado River gorge before the construction of the dam. Right, this photo was taken during dam construction from what today is the bottom of the lake!

Aerial picture of the new dam after the lake was formed.

The main picture shows Hoover Dam today.

CHAPTER 7

- **Las Vegas Helps the Military**

- **Training Air Force Pilots**

- **Magnesium for Bullets, Bombs, and Airplanes**

- **Testing Nuclear Bombs**

Las Vegas Helps the Military

Following the completion of Hoover Dam, Las Vegas faced an uncertain future once again. However, just a few years after many dam workers left Southern Nevada, the United States was drawn into World War II. Las Vegas had enough land around it to become important to the war effort. Whether it was training pilots, producing materials for weapons, or testing new weapons, Las Vegas helped protect the United States from its enemies.

Night firing practice on the moving target range at the Army airfield near Las Vegas in 1942.

Training Air Force Pilots

With so much barren land around Las Vegas, a small dirt runway north of Las Vegas made the perfect spot for Army pilots to learn how to shoot and drop bombs from their airplanes. The city of Las Vegas gave the Army Air Corps the runway and the land around it (back then, the Army and Navy had their own air forces; the U.S. Air Force was created after the war). The War Department eventually spent $2.5 million on airplane hangars, barracks for soldiers to live in, fuel stations, and three runways. Within nine months, the Army had created the largest air facility in the United States and Europe.

Unfortunately, the U.S. Congress didn't set aside enough money to buy guns for the training pilots. Pilots had to use BB guns and .22 rifles, which were cheap and available. In fact, the people of Las Vegas helped out by donating their own BB guns and rifles to the base.

The Thunderbirds, the Air Force's precision flying team, prepares for a flight in 1981. The team is based at Nellis Air Force Base.

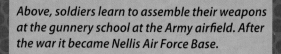

Above, soldiers learn to assemble their weapons at the gunnery school at the Army airfield. After the war it became Nellis Air Force Base.

At right, military personnel enjoy the Las Vegas clubs on their time off.

An airman inspects maintenance
on an aircraft at Nellis Air Force
Base. The airman originally had a
headquarters, as it looked in 1954.

As more men trained at the Army Air Corps base outside of Las Vegas, things improved. More guns were available. By the end of World War II, over 50,000 gunners and pilots had trained at the airbase.

After World War II, the training base was named **Nellis Air Force Base** after a World War II pilot from Searchlight, Nevada, who graduated from Las Vegas High School. William Nellis was shot down over France in World War II. He parachuted out of his plane and a French farmer rescued him. When he returned to safety, Nellis began flying again. Once again, he was shot down, this time over Belgium. Unfortunately, Nellis didn't survive the second time.

Nellis Air Force Base continues to train pilots. It remains an important part of the defense of the United States.

Lieutenant William Nellis

Magnesium for Bullets, Bombs, and Airplanes

Magnesium is a metal used in making bullets, bombs, and even planes. During World War II, so much magnesium was needed that the federal government built the largest magnesium factory in the world just outside of Las Vegas. It was a mile and three quarters long and three quarters of a mile wide. It was called the **Basic Magnesium Incorporated** plant.

The Basic Magnesium Plant Brings Water to Las Vegas

Since the Basic Magnesium plant needed so much water, the federal government put in large water pipes from Lake Mead to **Henderson**.

This meant the city of Las Vegas only needed to lay pipes from the Basic Magnesium plant to the city to get water from Lake Mead.

Without the Basic Magnesium plant, it would have been a long time before Lake Mead water reached Las Vegas. In the meantime, the Las Vegas Springs and the wells were drying up. It is possible that Las Vegas would have run out of water, if the Basic Magnesium plant had not been built.

The federal government chose Southern Nevada for this magnesium plant, because most of the magnesium ore came out of mines in Southern Nevada. Plus, Hoover Dam provided plenty of electricity for the plant. And most importantly, the large lake behind the dam, Lake Mead, had plenty of water for cooling the metal after it was refined and poured into molds for bullets, bombs, and airplane parts.

People working at Basic Magnesium Incorporated found hard work and difficult conditions. Most were happy to have the jobs. Bottom, construction of the Basic Magnesium plant employed local men.

Above, this woman molds ingots of magnesium. Left and below, women work to prepare finished ingots for shipment to arms and airplane manufacturers.

Since it was World War II, many of the men were fighting in different parts of the world. This left a limited number of men to work at the Basic Magnesium plant. Therefore, women took jobs that usually had been men's jobs, like driving forklifts and handling the hot metal, as it was poured into molds for bullets, bombs, and airplane parts. The women at the Basic Magnesium plant were known as "**Magnesium Maggies**."

In the summer, temperatures reached 130 degrees inside the factory. In the winter, temperatures fell to near freezing. Poisonous gasses and hot liquid metals surrounded the workers. The women worked in this dangerous place for up to 12 hours a day. The Magnesium Maggies showed that a woman could do what a man can do.

Basic Magnesium Incorporated hired 13,618 workers. That was more than 10 percent of the population of Nevada at the time. Unfortunately, there weren't enough houses for all those people. Campsites sprouted up along Boulder Highway, where people stayed in tents, trailers, or makeshift shacks.

During World War II, women were called upon for the first time to enter the workforce in large numbers, doing men's work in support of the war effort.

This boy was the first to attend Carver School in Henderson.

African Americans found work at the Basic Magnesium plant.

Left, the Williams family, first black family at Carver Park, pose in their doorway in 1943.

Below, black families lived in West Las Vegas' poor neighborhoods, like this one between C and D streets.

African Americans Find Work

When the Hoover Dam was being built, at first only white people were given jobs. Thanks to pressure from African Americans and some white officials who weren't racist, the dam's builder finally hired a few African Americans.

However, Basic Magnesium Incorporated hired people of all races. African Americans by the thousands moved to the Las Vegas Valley to work at the new plant. In 1940, there were only 178 African Americans living in the Las Vegas Valley. By 1950, there were 4,000 African Americans in the Las Vegas Valley.

While African Americans could work at the Basic Magnesium plant, they were not allowed to live in Las Vegas.

When Las Vegas was a brand new town, everyone who wasn't white lived in a single block known as block 17. Later, everyone who wasn't white was forced to live in West Las Vegas.

When the Basic Magnesium plant first started hiring African Americans, they had to live in West Las Vegas. However, there weren't enough houses and money to build new houses in West Las Vegas. So the plant built an area of Henderson for African Americans known as Carver Park.

When the Basic Magnesium plant closed, many people lost their jobs. Most African Americans went to work at the hotels.

Basic Magnesium Incorporated rushed to build houses for all the workers in what became known as Basic Townsite. Originally, they built the houses on wood planks so that when World War II was over, the houses could be dragged into Las Vegas. This didn't happen; instead, the houses remained and a new town was created. They named the new town **Henderson**, after former Senator Charles B. Henderson of Nevada. Among other achievements, Henderson did a lot to get the Basic Magnesium plant funded and built.

The Basic Magnesium plant did such a good job that within two years it had made enough magnesium for the rest of the war. So the federal government shut down the Basic Magnesium plant, and it became a chemical factory. Many people lost their jobs. In a short time, more than half the houses in Henderson were empty.

Fortunately, Las Vegas had a new industry: tourism. Soon, enough people were moving to Las Vegas to fill all the empty houses in Henderson and build new ones.

*A man stacks hot magnesium
ingots on pallets for shipment.*

Testing Nuclear Bombs

When World War II ended, Southern Nevada still had something to offer the military: lots of empty land. After World War II, the United States and the Soviet Union became involved in what was called the **Cold War**. The Cold War got its name because no real battle took place between the two countries. Instead, each side built up its military to keep the other side from attacking. Nuclear weapons were an important part of this build-up.

In 1951, a mysterious group of people checked into a hotel. These people slept only a few hours before getting up at 2:00 a.m. and driving north. A day or two later a blinding light flashed in the north and an odd looking cloud appeared.

The military tried to keep it a secret, but eventually the government had to admit that it was testing atom bombs at the new testing area in Mercury Springs, north of Las Vegas. To make people feel safe living so close to atom bomb explosions, the federal government invited reporters to the **Test Site**.

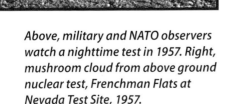

Above, military and NATO observers watch a nighttime test in 1957. Right, mushroom cloud from above ground nuclear test, Frenchman Flats at Nevada Test Site, 1957.

Since the government said it was safe, people flocked to Las Vegas to watch the atom bomb tests. The Las Vegas hotels were happy about the new tourist attraction. They gave guests special sunglasses to protect their eyes as they watched the explosions. They made boxed lunches for their guests to take outside with them on the day of blasts. They even created an atomic hairstyle for women.

Las Vegas benefited in other ways from the nuclear weapons testing. All the building materials and construction workers for the new Camp Mercury passed through Las Vegas. The payroll for construction brought more than $4 million into the Las Vegas area. The nuclear weapons testing also brought scientists, engineers, and other experts to live in Las Vegas.

Above, military observers and tourists gather at the official observation point to watch a daylight atomic bomb test. Below, atomic science fiction invades popular movies, comic books, toys, candy, and other consumer products during the 1940s and 1950s.

In 1963, the **Limited Test Ban Treaty** meant that nuclear tests moved underground. Instead of large, bright explosions that could be seen as far away as Los Angeles, the new tests caused underground rumbles.

In 1992, there was a ban on all nuclear weapons testing. This means the Test Site is no longer used for detonating nuclear weapons. Now the Department of Energy uses it for other purposes like training, weapons testing, and environmental studies. Before the 1992 nuclear weapons ban, there were 928 nuclear explosions at the Test Site. Today, scientific research continues at the Test Site, and millions of dollars still pour into the Las Vegas economy.

Sedan Crater was formed on July 6, 1962, during an underground test. The explosion blew 12 million tons of earth out of the crater. The crater is 320 feet deep and 1,280 feet in diameter.

Aerial view of test explosion craters at the Nevada Test Site. Sedan Crater can be seen near the top of the page. Inset, an above ground test in 1957.

CHAPTER 8

- **Building the Las Vegas Strip**

- **A Cop Builds the Pair-O-Dice**

- **El Rancho Becomes the First Resort on the Strip**

- **Griffith Builds the Last Frontier**

- **Criminals Come to the Strip**

Though the saloons and gentlemen's clubs below were not on the Strip, they began the tradition of entertainment halls in Las Vegas as far back as 1906. The "Welcome to Las Vegas" sign was installed in 1959 and still greets visitors to the Strip today.

Building the Las Vegas Strip

The tourists coming to see Hoover Dam and Lake Mead made people in Las Vegas more aware of the money that could be made from tourism. Besides the dam, lakes, and natural wonders, Las Vegas had something else to offer tourists: gambling.

The Desert Love Buggy was a familiar sight in annual Helldorado parades, a cowboy-themed celebration designed to lure tourists to Las Vegas.

While it seems like gambling has always been legal in Nevada, it was outlawed for many years. On October 1, 1910, a strict anti-gambling law took effect in Nevada that even outlawed flipping a coin. The law was only enforced for three weeks in Las Vegas. Soon people were gambling again in the saloons. The police ignored the gambling tables and slot machines.

Gambling became legal again in Nevada on March 19, 1931, when the state legislature realized how much money Nevadans could make from the tourists, who would want to come to Nevada to gamble. More and more, Las Vegas became a tourist town.

NITE CLUB

DINE & DANCE

One of the first gambling establishments, built and run by a policeman from Los Angeles, who gave the Strip its name.

GET CHANGE AT BAR

A Cop Builds the Pair-O-Dice

When **Guy McAfee** was a Los Angeles police officer, one of his duties was to bust illegal gambling parlors. However, he secretly ran illegal casinos himself. Eventually, he saw that owning a legal casino in Las Vegas would be easier.

McAfee bought a casino outside of the city limits on the highway to Los Angeles. He called his casino the **Pair-O-Dice**.

McAfee gets the credit for naming this stretch of road "the Strip" after the Sunset Strip in Los Angeles, where he used to work as a police officer. Of course, the lonely highway looked nothing like the glitzy Sunset Strip, but McAfee had a vision of what it would become.

The Pair-O-Dice casino didn't look anything like today's casinos. It was a simple building with none of the luxury and beauty casinos have today.

This type of slot machine was used by casinos in the 1940s.

El Rancho Becomes the First Resort on the Strip

Tom Hull built the first Las Vegas resort. He chose to build his resort on the highway leading to California, because there was plenty of inexpensive land. Like McAfee, he wanted to avoid paying city taxes and fees.

He paid an old woman $150 an acre for her land. The woman thought her land was worthless. She couldn't believe anyone would pay that much money for land along a dirt road that led into the desert.

Hull built a casino and small dining room surrounded by 65 guest cottages. He called the resort the **El Rancho Vegas**.

People didn't believe the El Rancho would be successful because it was so far out of town. Yet, it was the first resort on what is now called the Las Vegas Strip. Unfortunately, the El Rancho caught fire in 1960 and was totally destroyed.

The El Rancho Wagon Wheel Tavern served "chuck wagon" dinners, and was the model for today's mega buffets.

Above, the distinctive fence, sign, and weather vane of Hotel El Rancho Vegas. At right, El Rancho's rustic casino.

Griffith Builds the Last Frontier

Wheel of Fortune at the Last Frontier casino.

When **R. E. Griffith** came to Las Vegas and saw how successful the El Rancho was, he decided to build his own resort. Griffith purchased the Pair-O-Dice casino from Guy McAfee for $1,000 an acre. When Griffith handed over the $35,000 check, McAfee said, "If you'd bargained harder, I would've sold for less." Griffith's response was, "If you'd bargained harder, I would've paid more."

It turned out that paying for the land was the easiest part of building the new resort, called the **Last Frontier**. During World War II, the federal government was building a lot of new military bases. Since there was a shortage of building materials, the government rationed them, meaning that the few materials available were used for the military or important buildings. Casinos weren't considered important buildings.

When Griffith began building the Last Frontier, Army officials visited and took all the building materials to the new Army Air Corps training base on the edge of town, now called Nellis Air Force Base. The new resort could not be built without those materials, so Griffith bought two old mines and stripped them of their electrical wiring and other materials. He then sneaked the old materials to his property and continued building his resort.

The Last Frontier's unique sign. At far left, the casino.

The Last Frontier's pool was in the front, where it could attract the attention of passers-by.

At left, the Little Church of the West wedding chapel that Griffith built as part of the resort.

Since there was no modern air conditioning back then, the Last Frontier was built with little tunnels under the floor that carried cold water throughout the hotel. There were even cold water pipes in the walls of the rooms to keep them cool.

Unlike the El Rancho, which put its swimming pool in the back, Griffith put his pool out front. Then people driving along the hot and dusty highway would see it and want to stop at the Last Frontier to cool off.

Griffith also built a wedding chapel called the **Little Church of the West**. You still can see this chapel on Las Vegas Boulevard. It is all that is left of the Last Frontier.

From these humble resorts on a dirt highway heading into the desert arose one of the most famous stretches of resorts in the world — the Las Vegas Strip.

Last Frontier Village Las Vegas

7/3/52

Criminals Come to the Strip

While people wanted to build casinos in Las Vegas, banks didn't want to lend money to build them. Also, casinos were a new type of business and few people knew how to run them.

As it turns out, other people knew a lot about the gambling business and had a lot of money to invest. These men had, among other things, run illegal casinos throughout the United States. From all their criminal activities, they had plenty of money to invest. They were familiar with how much money can be made from gambling. The criminals formed groups that we sometime call "the Mafia" or "the Mob."

Al Capone, the boss of the Chicago mob in the 1920s, may have been interested in Las Vegas, but **Benjamin "Bugsy" Siegel** is probably the most well-known, or at least most visible, mobster in Las Vegas.

When Siegel came to Las Vegas in the 1940s, all of the resorts were western-style. But Siegel had a different vision for Las Vegas. He bought the resort that was being built on the Las Vegas Strip from William "Billy" Wilkerson, and turned it into the **Flamingo**. To make the Flamingo look

Pink flamingos were the trademark of the Flamingo Hotel and Casino, at right.

more like a Florida resort than a western one, it had a giant pink neon sign and fake pink flamingos on the lawn.

Siegel wanted to attract movie stars and wealthy people to his casino, so he poured money into carpets and furniture as well as the pool and tennis courts. To pay for all this luxury, Siegel borrowed from the mob.

Since these were violent men, Siegel was afraid they would try to kill him. He built the Flamingo like a fortress. Its concrete walls were reinforced with steel that came from the Navy. The top floor, where Siegel lived, had trap doors and escape hatches, one of which led to a getaway car in a secret garage.

All these luxuries and trap doors cost a lot of money. To make matters worse, people were stealing from Siegel. For instance, sometimes people would deliver building materials to the front gate and then drive out the back gate without unloading the materials. The next day, they would sell the same load to Siegel again.

The casino was supposed to cost $1.5 million, but the final cost was more than $6 million. The mobsters who loaned money to Siegel were not happy. Perhaps this is why Siegel was murdered six months after the Flamingo opened.

Benjamin "Bugsy" Siegel liked to dress the part of the classy, casino owning mobster.

Today the Flamingo looks nothing like it did when Siegel built it. Through the years, parts of the original hotel have been torn down and new towers built so that nothing is left of the original Flamingo.

Throughout the 1950s, many other people from organized crime were involved in building and running Las Vegas casinos. However, the Nevada government passed laws to make it more difficult for people with criminal records to own or operate casinos. But it wasn't just laws that got the Mafia out of Las Vegas; soon, wealthy men came to Las Vegas. These men bought the casinos from the Mafia and began running more honest businesses.

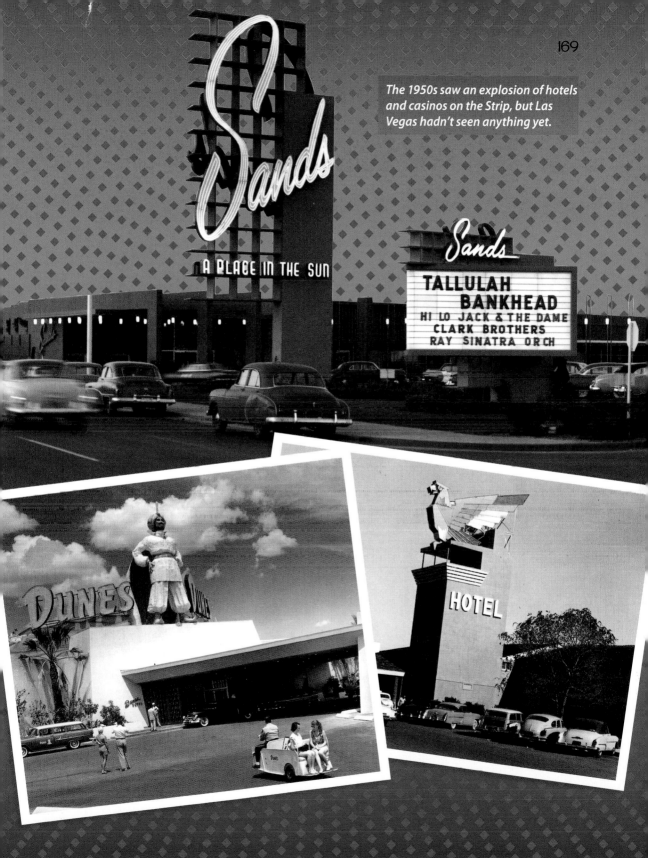

The 1950s saw an explosion of hotels and casinos on the Strip, but Las Vegas hadn't seen anything yet.

Sands

A PLACE IN THE SUN

Sands

TALLULAH
BANKHEAD
HI LO JACK & THE DAME
CLARK BROTHERS
RAY SINATRA ORCH

DUNES

HOTEL

CHAPTER 9

- **Las Vegas, Resort City of the West**

- **Howard Hughes Moves to Las Vegas**

- **Kerkorian Builds Casinos**

- **Wynn Changes the Strip**

- **The Springs Becomes a World-famous City**

Howard Hughes lived only four years in Las Vegas, but Summerlin was developed on land he owned, and is a lasting reminder of his time here. In this picture, Summerlin Parkway is under construction. Above, naturally landscaped parks meander through neighborhoods.

Las Vegas, Resort City of the West

Over the next fifty years Las Vegas would evolve, at times slowly, and other times seemingly overnight. The city remade itself from sleepy desert town, to glitzy nightspot, to family vacation mecca, to the home of the mega entertainment fantasy land. In 1960, the era of hotel implosions and giant construction projects was yet to come—and it was coming soon.

Howard Hughes Moves to Las Vegas

When **Howard Hughes** secretly arrived in Las Vegas on a train in 1966, he had just sold his airline company. This sale not only made Hughes the wealthiest man in the world, but also meant that he received the largest check ever written to a single person: $546,549,171. Hughes needed to invest his money and avoid paying millions in taxes, and he chose Las Vegas as the place he would live while investing his fortune.

While very successful, Hughes acted oddly. His many strange behaviors included an extreme fear of germs. As a result, he locked himself away. He rarely left his room or allowed people to visit him.

When Hughes arrived in Las Vegas, he rented the two top floors of the Desert Inn for 10 days. However, when the 10 days were up, he didn't leave. Of course the owners were not happy. Other guests were supposed to stay in the rooms where Hughes was living. These other guests would spend a lot more money on gambling than Hughes, who was too afraid of germs to leave his room. To keep from having to move out of the Desert Inn, Hughes bought the hotel for $13.2 million.

Hughes stands with his airplane after a night landing. He had crashed this plane the previous year. At left, he pilots his famous "sky boat," known as the Spruce Goose.

The Landmark

Once Hughes heard how much money he could make with this new casino, he said, "How many more of these toys are available? Let's buy them all." Over the next few months Hughes bought four more casinos. He even bought one casino just because its sign disturbed his sleep.

Hughes also built the **Landmark** Hotel-Casino. This casino was a tower with what looked like a flying saucer on top of it. The building reached 31 stories, making it the tallest building in Las Vegas at the time. However, this odd-looking building didn't have many rooms and it only had a small casino. It never was successful and was later destroyed.

Hughes bought a local airport and a television station. He also tried to move his aircraft company to Las Vegas. He owned 25,000 acres of land north and west of Las Vegas. However, the people who worked for him did not want to move from California to the desert. The property later became Summerlin. This community was named after Hughes' grandmother, Jean Amelia Summerlin.

Howard Hughes also had investments and interests in film making through his company, RKO Radio Pictures.

One day, Hughes read a newspaper story about a hydrogen bomb test that was going to happen at the testing grounds. The article warned that people might feel earth tremors following the explosion.

This story bothered Hughes. At first, he tried to bribe President Lyndon B. Johnson and presidential candidates Richard M. Nixon and Hubert H. Humphrey with a $100,000 each to end nuclear testing in Southern Nevada. Even though Nixon and Humphrey both took the money for their campaigns, the nuclear testing continued. Discouraged, Hughes decided to leave Las Vegas.

On Thanksgiving Day, four years after coming to Las Vegas, Hughes sneaked out of town. No one noticed for nearly a week that he had left. Even then, no one knew where he had gone. Later they found out Hughes was living in the Bahamas.

Hughes did more for Las Vegas than buy casinos. His example showed other wealthy business people that Las Vegas casinos were a good investment. Soon other business people were buying and building casinos with Las Vegas quickly growing and becoming an even more popular place to visit.

Hughes warms up his XF-11 for a test flight. It was one of the world's fastest photographic spy planes.

Thunderbird Hotel

NAT "KING" COLE AND THE TRIO
ALSO BUNNY BRIGGS
DANSATIONS CHUCK GOULD&ORCH

Though famed crooner Nat King Cole headlined at the Thunderbird Hotel, he could not stay there.

Whites Only

In the early days, only white people were allowed into casinos and hotels. Even famous and talented African American entertainers and musicians could not stay in the hotels or eat in the restaurants. They had to stay in West Las Vegas.

It took threats of protests in the 1950s and 1960s to get the major casinos to open their doors to all races to avoid negative publicity, and then to agree to hire African Americans for good jobs. Now casinos are open to everyone.

INTERNATIONAL

JULIET PROWSE
breathes fire into
MAME!

LION
MAIN
SHOWROOM

The International was the largest
building on the Strip when it was
built. At right, headliner Elvis Presley
appeared here for several years.

Kerkorian Builds Casinos

Kirk Kerkorian is called the "father of the mega-resort." People call him this because his focus on entertainment and large resorts started a new era in Las Vegas.

Kerkorian was a pilot who flew people from Los Angeles to Las Vegas. By buying and selling used airplanes, Kerkorian was able to raise enough money to start a small airline.

In 1968, Kerkorian sold his airline and bought the Flamingo. He also bought 82 acres on Paradise Road to build his own casino, The International. While Howard Hughes' Landmark hotel was slightly taller, the International was the largest hotel in the world — at least until Kerkorian built his next one.

People thought The International would fail because it had too many rooms (1,512). They also said it was too far away from the Strip. But Kerkorian hired big stars like Elvis Presley and Barbra Streisand to sing and entertain his guests, and people flocked to The International. The International was so successful that Hilton Hotels bought it renaming it the Hilton Hotel and Casino.

Kirk Kerkorian, the father of the mega-resort.

After selling The International and the Flamingo, Kerkorian bought the MGM movie studios. He then built the world's largest casino, larger than the Hilton. He named his new casino **MGM Grand**. This hotel wasn't the MGM Grand we have today. The original MGM Grand is now called Bally's.

After selling the old MGM Grand to Bally's, Kerkorian went on to build an even larger casino. The current MGM Grand has more than 5,000 rooms.

The MGM Grand is now a **public company**, which means many people own a share of the company. While Kerkorian continued to own many of the shares, he was not the only owner. Kerkorian's money and the money from the other owners made it possible for the MGM Grand to build and begin buying other casinos. Today, MGM Mirage owns many of the major casinos on the Strip.

This enormous lion guards the entrance to the new MGM Grand.

Fire at the MGM Grand

The original MGM Grand was the site of Las Vegas' biggest disaster.

On November 21, 1980, an electrical problem started a fire at seven o'clock one morning. A server saw flames coming out of a keno machine and sounded an alarm.

Soon smoke traveled through doorways, stairways, and heating ducts. When it reached the top of the casino, the smoke rose nearly one mile into the sky.

Eighty-seven people died in the MGM Grand fire.

A helicopter rescues a hotel guest from the top of the building. Black smoke spreads over the city, blocking the sun. Right, fire trucks bring help.

The Mirage offers free entertainment for those passing by. On the Mirage's opening day, thousands of visitors streamed through the gates.

Wynn Changes the Strip

Steve Wynn's vision of the mega-resort changed the Las Vegas Strip forever. Casinos are no longer simple hotels with gambling in the lobby. Instead, casinos now have many attractions, amazing shows, and even roller coasters.

Wynn came to Las Vegas when he was only 10 years old and dreamed of coming back as an adult. When he did, he was able to buy land next to Caesars Palace. He sold that land to make money to buy a casino. Finally, in 1989, Wynn opened the most expensive casino ever: the Mirage, up the street from Caesars.

The Mirage offered things people hadn't seen in a hotel-casino, such as dolphins and white tigers. In front of the casino, he built a waterfall and a volcano that erupts fire.

It cost so much to build the Mirage that the casino had to make $1 million a day to pay its bills. People thought there wouldn't be enough visitors to support the new casino, but Wynn proved them wrong. In one year, the Mirage replaced Hoover Dam as the leading tourist attraction in Nevada.

Steve Wynn

Spectators gaze at the beauty of the Bellagio fountains.

In fact, so many people visited the Mirage, Wynn built another casino next to it called Treasure Island (now called TI). This casino had a pirate show in front of the hotel that included the sinking of one of the ships.

A few years later, Wynn built the Bellagio. In front of this casino, Wynn put an amazing water show unlike any fountain that people had seen before. This casino also cost more than any other casino ($1.6 billion).

MGM eventually bought all of Wynn's casinos. Wynn went on to purchase the Desert Inn as a birthday present for his wife. He blew up the Desert Inn and built the Wynn Las Vegas Resort in its place.

First, the Mirage was the most expensive casino to be built. Then the Bellagio was the most expensive casino. When the Wynn casino was built, it was the most expensive casino, costing $1 billion more than the Bellagio cost.

Wynn and his success inspired a building boom that created the Las Vegas Strip we see today. Other people built the Stratosphere, the Excalibur, the New York-New York, the Luxor, the Venetian, the Paris, the Mandalay Bay, and others. Las Vegas became a city like no other in the world.

Treasure Island's pirate ship goes down in flames to thrill tourists. Below, the Wynn Las Vegas Resort takes shape under Wynn's watchful eye.

The Springs Becomes a World-famous City

A group of springs in a lonely desert became a city known around the world. From its humble beginnings of camps and small ranches, close to two million people now call Las Vegas their home. Where once barren land stretched to the mountains, houses now cover the desert. While only a small amount of water still comes from the Las Vegas Springs, the springs still nourish the soul of Las Vegas. Once Helen Stewart had to hire a teacher just for her children; now, about 300,000 students attend public and private schools in Southern Nevada.

Las Vegas has become more than a small desert town; it is now a famous city. The springs in a desolate desert have become the destination of visitors from around the world. Thousands of people from Asia, Africa, Europe, South America, Australia and all the corners of the world travel to the entertainment capital of the world.

By day or by night, the Strip dazzles all who see it.

Imagine a dusty, thirsty explorer from 150 years ago traveling across the hot desert. Imagine him running to the Las Vegas Springs to drink from the warm water and relax in the shade of a cottonwood tree. Now imagine telling him about all the people who would live in Las Vegas, and the houses that would cover the valley. Imagine telling him about people flying from around the world to visit a city of neon lights. And imagine telling him about things like the Bellagio fountains, the Stratosphere Tower, and the Fremont Street Experience.

The explorer probably would think you had gone crazy from being in the desert too long. He would not understand how lovely springs in a lonely desert could become such a beautiful and popular place to live and visit. But you know the history of Las Vegas and what made it the city it is today. You could tell that explorer from the past the amazing story of how the springs in the desert became a world-famous city.

Glossary

adobe: a sun-baked brick made of clay and straw.

archeologist: a person who studies the lives, customs, and times of ancient people.

artifacts: anything made by human skill, especially tools or weapons.

Armijo, Antonio: a Mexican who wanted to find a shortcut to California that would save time by cutting across the desert and mountains.

Anasazi: Indians who lived 2,000 years ago in Southern Nevada, New Mexico, and Arizona.

auction: a public sale where land was sold to the person who offered the most money for it.

bankrupt: unable to pay debt; must sell property or possessions to pay people money owed.

Basic Magnesium Incorporated: a plant where magnesium ore was refined and made into bullets, bombs, and airplane parts.

Blue Room: the name for a Las Vegas jail.

Boulder City: a town near Hoover Dam.

Clark, Senator William: a railroad man, who was an early land developer in the Las Vegas area.

Cold War: a struggle after World War II where each side built up its military to keep the other side from attacking.

collateral: property promised as security for a loan.

conservation: conserving, preserving, and protecting from loss or waste.

county seat: the town or city where the government of a county is located.

El Rancho Vegas: the first resort on the Las Vegas Strip built by Tom Hull.

evaporate: to give off moisture.

Flamingo: a large hotel resort on the Las Vegas Strip built by the well-known mobster, Benjamin "Bugsy" Siegel.

Fremont, John C.: an early American explorer, who visited the Las Vegas Valley.

Gass, Octavius Decatur "O. D.": early Las Vegas settler who made a fortune selling food and supplies to the miners at his Las Vegas Ranch.

Great Depression: a period from 1929 to 1939 where many people did not have jobs.

Griffith, R. E.: builder of the Last Frontier, a hotel resort on the Las Vegas Strip, during World War II.

Henderson: a town near the Basic Magnesium Incorporated plant named after State Senator Charles B. Henderson.

hobos: people who wander about and live by begging or doing odd jobs.

Hoover Dam: a large dam on the Colorado River that was the tallest in the world when it was built.

Hughes, Howard: one of the wealthiest men in the world, who bought the Desert Inn and many other hotels and casinos in Las Vegas.

Hull, Tom: built the first resort, the El Rancho Vegas, on the Las Vegas Strip.

"Journada de Muerta" or **Journey of Death:** a 55-mile stretch of desert, between the Muddy River and Las Vegas Springs, that had no water.

Lake Mead: a large lake formed behind Hoover Dam.

Landmark: a large hotel-casino resort built by Howard Hughes.

Las Vegas: Spanish word that means "the meadows."

Last Frontier: a hotel resort on the Las Vegas Strip built by R. E. Griffith during World War II.

lice: a small, wingless insect that infests the hair or skin of people.

Limited Test Ban Treaty: moved all nuclear testing underground, causing underground rumbles.

Little Church of the West: a wedding chapel at the Last Frontier.

Kerkorian, Kirk: the "father of the mega-resort," who built the International and the MGM Grand.

magnesium: a light, silver-white metal used in making bullets, bombs, and even planes.

Magnesium Maggies: women who worked at the Basic Magnesium Incorporated plant during World War II.

McAfee, Guy: developed the first casino, the Pair-O-Dice, outside the city limits on the Strip.

McWilliams, J. T.: started Ragtown located just north of where the Spaghetti Bowl is today in West Las Vegas.

metates: grinding stones.

MGM Grand: the world's largest casino, which has more than 5,000 rooms.

moonshiners: persons who make illegal alcohol.

Mormon Church: a religious group that settled in Salt Lake City, Utah.

Mormon Fort: a fort the Mormons built, where Las Vegas is now, that was 150 feet by 150 feet with adobe walls that were 14 feet high.

Nellis Air Force Base: a military base outside of Las Vegas where Air Force pilots are trained.

Old Spanish Trail: the trail that went through Southern Nevada connecting Santa Fe, New Mexico, with Los Angeles, California.

ore: a mineral or rock containing metal.

Pair-O-Dice: a casino on "the Strip" named and owned by Guy McAfee.

Paiute: a small tribe of Indians living in Nevada, Utah, California, and Arizona.

Paleo-Indians: prehistoric Indians who migrated from Asia to the Americas.

petroglyphs: pictures carved into rocks.

public company: a business or company in which many people own a share.

Ragtown: a city of tents began by J. T. McWilliams, which later became known as West Las Vegas.

Rivera, Rafael: a teenager, who was the first non-Indian to visit the Las Vegas Valley on January 7, 1829.

Siegel, Benjamin "Bugsy:" a well-known mobster who built the Flamingo resort on the Las Vegas Strip.

Stewart, Archibald: a man who got the Las Vegas Ranch in 1881, as payment on the O. D. Gass loan.

Stewart, Helen: inherited the Las Vegas Ranch upon the murder of her husband, Archibald Stewart, and became known as the "First Lady of Las Vegas."

strike: workers join together and refuse to work until their demands are met.

survey: measure for size, shape, position, or boundaries.

Test Site: an area in Mercury Springs, north of Las Vegas, where atomic bombs were tested.

utilities: companies that perform a public services like water, electric, and gas.

wickiups: small huts made of willow branches, grass, and sagebrush used by the Indians in summer.

Williams, Tom: built a new town known as "Old Town" that is now North Las Vegas.

Wynn, Steve: built the Mirage, Treasure Island, Bellagio, and the Wynn Las Vegas Resort.

Bibliography

Ainlay, Thomas "Taj" Jr. and Judy Dixon Gabaldon. *Las Vegas: The Fabulous First Century*. Charleston, SC: Arcadia Publishing, 2003.

BeDunnah, Gary. *Discovering Nevada*. Salt Lake City: Gibbs Smith Publisher, 1994.

Hopkins, A.D. and K.J. Evans, editors. *The First 100: Portraits of the Men and Women Who Shaped Las Vegas*. Las Vegas: Huntington Press, 1999.

Land, Barbara and Myrick Land. *A Short History of Las Vegas, Second Edition*. Reno: University of Nevada Press, 2004.

Moehring, Eugene P. and Michael S. Green. *Las Vegas: A Centennial History*. Reno: University of Nevada Press, 2005.

Paher, Stanley W. *Las Vegas: As it Began – As it Grew*. Las Vegas: Nevada Publications, 1971.

Whitely, Joan Burkhart. *Young Las Vegas: Before the Future Found Us*. Las Vegas: Stephens Press, 2005.

Wright, Frank. *Nevada Yesterdays: Short Looks at Las Vegas History*. Las Vegas: Stephens Press, 2005.

About the Author

Jonathan Peters, Ph.D. is a professional writer from Las Vegas. He holds a doctorate in American Studies and is an adjunct professor at the University of Nevada, Las Vegas. When he adopted Las Vegas as his home, Dr. Peters developed a deep interest in the people and history of the area. He is just as comfortable traversing the unpopulated areas of Southern Nevada as he is visiting with tourists on the Las Vegas Strip.

Photograph and Illustration Credits

Cover illustration:

The Las Vegas Springs by Laura Marshall

Front matter:

Half-title and title pages: illustration by Laura Marshall

Page 5: Los Vegas Rancho, illustration by Frederick S. Dellenbaugh, used with permission from Nevada State Museum & Historical Society

Pages 6-7: Las Vegas Centennial Mural, used with permission, Nancy Imada, teacher, Hillcrest Academy, Las Vegas, Nevada

Pages 8-9: Mohave Indian Pottery, photo by E.L. Curtis; Hoover Dam, used with permission, ©2005 David Andrew Gilder; The Last Frontier; Vegas Vic Postcard reproduced with permission from Nevada State Museum & Historical Society, *Nevada Yesterdays* (Stephens Press, LLC, 2005); Las Vegas Strip, photo by Jon Sullivan

Chapter 1. The First Las Vegas Visitors

Pages 10-11: Desert Landscape, illustration used with permission, from Roy Purcell

Pages 12-13: Mammoth, illustration by Eldon Doty

Page 14: Bighorns; Equus Pacificus, photos by Carolyn Hayes Uber; Equus Pacificus drawing by Melissa Rogers

Page 15: Giant Sloth, illustration by Kathryn Hunley

Pages 16-17: Petroglyphs, used with permission from Nevada Rock Art Foundation, ©2004

Page 17: Pictograms, by Roy Purcell, reproduced with permission, *Long Journey from Wikame* (Stephens Press, LLC, 2006)

Page 18: Anasazi, by Kathryn Hunley; Pit House Diagram, used with permission from Lost City Museum

Page 19: Mano and Metate, photo by Carolyn Hayes Uber

Pages 20-21: Lost City photos, used with permission from UNLV Libraries, Special Collections; Lake Mead, photo by Fran Miles

Pages 22-23: Paiute illustration by Mike Miller reproduced with permission, *Tales for Tomás* (Stephens Press, LLC, 2005); Agave, photo by Gary Unwin

Page 24: Wikiup, used with permission from UNLV Libraries, Special Collections; Washoe baskets, photo by Carolyn Hayes Uber

Page 25: Paiute family, by Roy Purcell, reproduced with permission, *Long Journey from Wikame* (Stephens Press, LLC, 2006)

Chapter 2. Explorers Discover the Las Vegas Valley

Pages 26-27: Mexican blankets, photo by Jill Fromer

Page 28: Statue of Rivera, used with permission, photo by Mike Salsbury, *Las Vegas Review-Journal*

Page 29: Ox cart, photo by Tim Pleasant

Page 30: Spaniards, illustration by Mike Miller, reproduced with permission, *Tales for Tomás* (Stephens Press, LLC, 2005)

Page 31: Spanish Trail Map, by Roy Purcell, used with permission, *Las Vegas, As it Began—As it Grew,* (Nevada Publications, 1971)

Pages 32-33: Rivera, illustration by Kathryn Hunley

Pages 34-35: Cutting cows, illustration by Eldon Doty

Page 36: John C. Fremont, courtesy of University of South Florida

Pages 36-37: Big Springs, used with permission from UNLV Libraries, Special Collections

Page 37: Old books, photo by Paul Cowan

Chapter 3. Settlers Move to the Las Vegas Valley

Pages 38-39: Old Morman Fort, illustration by Merv Corning, used with permission, *Las Vegas, As it Began—As it Grew,* (Nevada Publications, 1971)

Page 40: Mormon settlers, illustration by Mike Miller reproduced with permission, *Tales for Tomás* (Stephens Press, LLC, 2005)

Page 41: Camp cooking, photo by Scott Leigh

Pages 42-43: Journada de Muerta, illustration by Eldon Doty

Page 44: Wooden bucket, photo by Stephen Rothe

Pages 44-45: Ranch site, used with permission from UNLV Libraries, Special Collections

Pages 46-47: Old Fort, photos by Carolyn Hayes Uber

Page 48: Working for squash, illustration by Kathryn Hunley

Page 49: Squash, photo by Pierre Jansen; Desert squash, illustration, used with permission from Roy Purcell

Page 50: Old bullets, photo by Aanssi Ruuska

Page 51 Potosi Mine courtesy of U.S. Geological Survey; Old miner and donkeys, used with permission from UNLV Libraries Special collections

Pages 52-53: Mining, illustration by Mike Miller reproduced with permission, *Tales for Tomás* (Stephens Press, LLC, 2005); Mine hoist and tools, photo by Carolyn Hayes Uber

Page 54: Book of Mormon, photo by Carolyn Hayes Uber

Page 55: Interior of Fort, used with permission, photo by Ralph Fountain, *Las Vegas Review-Journal*

Chapter 4. Ranchers Live in the Las Vegas Valley

Pages 56-57: Los Vegas Rancho, illustration by Frederick S. Dellenbaugh, used with permission, Nevada State Historical Soiety & Museum

Page 58: Miners and Burros, illustration by Eldon Doty

Page 59: Burro train, used with permission from UNLV Libraries, Special Collections

Page 60: O.D. Gass; Mary Virginia Gass, used with permission, *Las Vegas, As it Began—As it Grew,* (Nevada Publications, 1971)

Page 61: Las Vegas Ranch Map, used with permission from Roy Purcell; Old Fort Stockade, used with permission, photo by Ralph Fountain, *Las Vegas Review-Journal*

Page 62: Gass and Warriors, illustration by Eldon Doty

Page 63: Pinto beans, photo by Ed Endicott

Pages 64-65: Valley ranchland, illustration, used with permission from Roy Purcell

Page 66: Photos of Stewart Ranch, all; Portraits: Archibald Stewart; Helen Stewart, used with permission from UNLV Libraries, Special Collections

Page 67: C. Kiel, illustration by Susan Keller

Page 68: Paiute Annie; Paiute man, used with permission from UNLV Libraries, Special Collections

Page 69: Little girl dancers; Young boy dancer, photos by Amy Beth Bennett; used with permission, *Las Vegas Review-Journal*; Grandfather and tiny dancer, photo by Shelly Donahue, *Las Vegas Review-Journal*

Pages 70-71: Train, illustration by Susan Keller

Page 71 Railroad map, illustration, used with permission from Roy Purcell

Page 72: Clark on train, used with permission from UNLV Libraries, Special Collections

Page 73: Train car depot, used with permission from UNLV Libraries, Special Collections

Chapter 5. The City of Las Vegas is Born

Pages 74-75: Auction of Clark Townsite; used with permission from Nevada State Historical Society & Museum; Clark Townsite Map, used with permission from UNLV Libraries, Special Collections

Page 76: Depot plans; Depot viewed from Fremont; Depot ladies, used with permission from UNLV Libraries, Special Collections

Page 77: Plaza Hotel, used with permission, photo by Jane Kalinowsky, *Las Vegas Review-Journal*

Page 78: Auctioneer photo, used with permission from UNLV Libraries, Special Collections

Pages 78-79: Land Auction, illustration by Mike Miller reproduced with permission, *Tales for Tomás* (Stephens Press, LLC, 2005)

Page 79: Railroad lantern, photo by Sue Campbell

Pages 80-81: Tent hotel; Tent home, used with permission from UNLV Libraries, Special Collections

Page 81: Tents by creek, used with permission from UNLV Libraries, Special Collections

Page 82: Fremont St. Experience, used with permission photo by Jerry Henkel, *Las Vegas Review-Journal*

Page 83: Bed in tent; Chop houses, used with permission from UNLV Libraries, Special Collections

Page 84: First School; Early class; Girls basketball, used with permission from UNLV Libraries, Special Collections

Page 86: Faucet photo by Ayala Studio, Lizard rendering by Linda Bucklin

Page 87: Desert cooler, illustration by Thomson Digital

Pages 88-89: Burros in street, illustration by Eldon Doty

Page 90: Spaghetti Bowl, courtesy of Nevada Department of Transportation

Page 91: Las Vegas Townsite ad; Gushing well, used with permission from UNLV Libraries, Special Collections

Page 92: McWilliams Town, used with permission from UNLV Libraries, Special Collections

Page 92-93: Crowd at McWilliams Town, used with permission from UNLV Libraries, Special Collections

Page 94: Ice tongs, photo by Pierrette Guertin; Vintage ice sign, photo by MBC Design Studio; Blocks of ice, photo by Diane Diederich

Page 95: Ice wagon; First ice plant, used with permission from UNLV Libraries, Special Collections

Page 96-97: Monroe St., used with permission from UNLV Libraries, Special Collections

Page 96: Underpass on Bonanza, used with permission, *Las Vegas Review-Journal*

Page 98: Tom Williams at gas pump, used with permission from UNLV Libraries, Special Collections

Page 99: Tom Williams and wife, used with permission from UNLV Libraries, Special Collections

Page 100: Las Vegas Laundry, used with permission from UNLV Libraries, Special Collections

Page 101: Moonshiners, illustration by Kathryn Hunley

Page 102: Clark County map, illustration, used with permission from Roy Purcell

Chapter 6. Hoover Dam Saves Las Vegas

Pages 126-127, Hoover Dam, used with permission, © 2005 David Andrew Gilder

Page 126: Black Canyon; Dam from lake bottom, used with permission from UNLV Libraries, Special Collections

Page 127: Aerial of Dam, used with permission from UNLV Libraries, Special Collections

Chapter 7. Las Vegas Helps the Military

Pages 128-129: USAF Thunderbirds, courtesy of USAF Thunderbirds

Page 130: Nellis guard, illustration by Mike Miller reproduced with permission, *Tales for Tomás* (Stephens Press, LLC, 2005)

Page 131: Night gunnery training, courtesy of Nevada State Museum & Historical Society

Page 132: Thunderbirds insignia, courtesy of USAF Thunderbirds; Thunderbird jets on ground, used with permission from UNLV Libraries, Special Collections

Page 133: Gunnery school; Soldiers at Last Frontier, used with permission from UNLV Libraries, Special Collections

Page 134: Airplane maintenance, courtesy of USAF Thunderbirds; Nellis Air Force Base Headquarters, used with permission from UNLV Libraries, Special Collections

Page 135: Lt. William Nellis, courtesy of United States Air Force

Page 136: Pipe and faucet, illustration, by Julie Felton

Page 137: Construction of BMI; BMI workers, used with permission from UNLV Libraries, Special Collections

Page 138: Woman worker at BMI; BMI Lady with ingots; BMI Ladies, used with permission from UNLV Libraries, Special Collections

Page 139: Good Work Sister, courtesy, U.S. Library of Congress, Prints and Photographs Division

Page 140: Boy at Carver School; Williams family; African American worker, used with permission from UNLV Libraries, Special Collections

Pages 140-141: C and D Streets, used with permission from UNLV Libraries, Special Collections

Page 142: House illustration by Dennis Cox; Tow truck illustration by Murat Bozkurt

Page 143: Man handles hot ingots, used with permission from UNLV Libraries, Special Collections

Page 144: Nuclear test NATO observers, photo courtesy of National Nuclear Security Administration, Nevada Site Office

Page 145: Red mushroom cloud, used with permission from UNLV Libraries, Special Collections

Page 146: Atomic tourists, illustration by Eldon Doty

Page 147: Observers at daylight test, photo courtesy of National Nuclear Security Administration, Nevada Site Office

Page 147: "Atomic" consumer products, courtesy, Oak Ridge Associated Universities' Health Physics Historical Instrumentation Museum Collection

Page 148: Sedan Crater, photo courtesy of National Nuclear Security Administration, Nevada Site Office

Page 149: Aerial view of craters, photo courtesy of National Nuclear Security Administration, Nevada Site Office; Scenic mushroom cloud, used with permission from UNLV Libraries, Special Collections

Chapter 8. Building the Las Vegas Strip

Pages 150-151: Roulette wheel, photo by Irochka Tischenko

Page 152: Welcome sign, photo by David Fox; Block 16 clubs; Arizona Club, used with permission from UNLV Libraries, Special Collections

Page 153: Desert Love Buggy, used with permission from UNLV Libraries, Special Collections

Page 154-155: Pitching coins, illustration by Kathryn Hunley

Page 156: Poker chips, photo by George Clerk; Pair-O-Dice, used with permission from UNLV Libraries, Special Collections; Inside a casino, courtesy U.S. Library of Congress, War Information Division, photo by Arthur Rothstein

Page 158: Wagon Wheel Tavern, used with permission from UNLV Libraries, Special Collections; Buffet, photo by Franklin Lugenbeel

Page 159: El Rancho sign; El Rancho casino interior, used with permission from UNLV Libraries, Special Collections

Pages 160-161: Last Frontier Wheel of Fortune; Last Frontier sign, used with permission from UNLV Libraries, Special Collections

Page 162: Last Frontier pool; Little Church of the West, used with permission from UNLV Libraries, Special Collections

Page 163: Last Frontier Village, used with permission from UNLV Libraries, Special Collections

Pages 164-165: Plastic flamingos, photo by Stan Rohrer; Flamingo pool, used with permission from UNLV Libraries, Special Collections

Page 166: Bugsy escapes, illustration by Eldon Doty

Page 167: Benjamin "Bugsy" Siegel, courtesy of Security Pacific Collection; Los Angeles Public Library

Page 168: Money bag, photo by Stefan Klein

Page 169: The Sands; The Dunes; The Thunderbird, used with permission from UNLV Libraries, Special Collections

Chapter 9. Las Vegas Resort City of the West

Page 170-171: Strip at night, photo by John Gurzinski, used with permission, *Las Vegas Review-Journal*

Page 172: Summerlin parkway, photo by Jeff Scheid, used with permission, *Las Vegas Review-Journal*; Pueblo Park, used with permission, *Las Vegas Mercury*

Page 174: Do Not Disturb, photo by Stephen Coburn

Page 175: Hughes/flashlight; Flying boat, used with permission from UNLV Libraries, Special Collections

Page 176: Landmark hotel, photo by Toru Kawana, used with permission, *Las Vegas Review-Journal*

Page 177: Hughes/films, used with permission from UNLV Libraries, Special Collections

Page 178: Hughes/XF-11, used with permission from UNLV Libraries, Special Collections

Page 179: Thunderbird marquee, used with permission from UNLV Libraries, Special Collections; Nat King Cole, used with permission from *Las Vegas Review-Journal*, courtesy of Capital Records Photo Archives

Page 180: International, photo by Terry Todd, used with permission from *Las Vegas Review-Journal*; Young Elvis, courtesy U.S. Library of Congress.

Page 181: Kerk Kerkorian, used with permission from *Las Vegas Review-Journal*

Page 182: MGM lion, photo by Jon Sullivan

Page 183: Helicopter rescue, photo by Gary Thompson; MGM black smoke, photo by Scott Henry; MGM fire/firetruck, used with permission from *Las Vegas Review-Journal*

Page 184: Mirage Volcano; Mirage opening, used with permission from *Las Vegas Review-Journal*

Page 185: Steve Wynn, photo by John Gurzinski, used with permission from *Las Vegas Review-Journal*

Page 186: Bellagio fountains, photo by Jane Kalinowsky, used with permission from *Las Vegas Review-Journal*; Bellagio fountains from above, photo by Jon Sullivan

Page 187: TI pirate ship; TI pirate ship sinks, photos by Jon Sullivan

Page 187: Wynn construction, used with permission from *Las Vegas Review-Journal*

Page 188: The Strip by night, photo by Jon Sullivan

Page 189: The Strip by day, photo by Jon Sullivan

Page 191: Old timer on the Strip, illustration by Eldon Doty

Page 192-193: Drive Carefully sign, photo by William Diaz Rex

Page 198: Jonathan Peters, photo courtesy of the author

For Teachers and Parents

Springs in the Desert: A Kid's History of Las Vegas has a companion book, *Springs in the Desert Activity Book*. The purpose of the activity book is to expand learning with activities. The activities may be implemented in the classroom, at home, or in the community either as group or individual experiences. It encourages students to become involved in exploring and experiencing the history, the environment, the culture, and the political structure of the greater Las Vegas area. It is based on the premise that democracy does not simply exist, but that it is participatory. It encourages involvement in the community. Today's learning environment is very closely tied to the Internet for basic information and research. This book reflects this trend and provides many different web sites to extend and enhance the learning experience. When an actual trip to an historic site, museum, or park is not possible, a "virtual trip" may be experienced on-line. All sites were tested at the time of publication.

 Springs in the Desert Activity Book provides essential concepts, skill and experiences to meet the **Nevada Social Studies Standards** in the areas of Civics, Economics, Geography, and History. More information on the Nevada Content and Performance Standards for Social Studies may be found on-line at http://www.doe.nv.gov/standards/socialstudies. The learning experiences in this book are closely aligned with the **Clark County School District Curriculum Essentials Framework**. The Clark County School District provides a Curriculum Overview for parents on-line at http://ccsd.net/cpd/curriculumpdfs/elem3-5.pdf.

Nevada Social Studies Standards addressed in the Activity book include:
Civics:

1.0: Rules, Laws, and Government : Students know why society needs rules, laws, and governments.

4.0: Political Process: Students describe the roles of political parties, interest groups, and public opinion in the democratic process.

6.0: State and Local Government: Students know the structure and functions of state and local governments.

Economics:

1.0: The Economic Way of Thinking: Students will use fundamental economic concepts, including, scarcity, choice, cost incentives, and costs versus benefits to describe and analyze problems and opportunities, both individual and social.

7.0: An Evolving Economy: Students will demonstrate an understanding of how investments, entrepreneurship, competition, and specialization lead to changes in an economy's structure and performance.

Geography:

1.0: The World in Spatial Terms: Students use maps, globes, and other geographic tools and technologies to locate and derive information about people, places, and environments.

2.0: Places and Regions: Students understand the physical and human features and cultural characteristics of places and use this information to define and study regions and their patterns of changes.

3.0: Physical Systems: Students understand how physical processes shape Earth's surface patterns and ecosystems.

4.0: Human Systems: Students understand how economic, political, and cultural processes interact to shape patterns of human migration and settlement, influence and interdependence, and conflict and cooperation.

5.0: Environment and Society: Students understand the effects of interactions between human and physical systems and the changes in use, distribution, and importance of resources.

6.0: Geographic Applications: Students apply geographic knowledge of people, places, and environments to interpret the past, understand the present, and plan for the future.

History:

1.0: Chronology: Students use chronology to organize and understand the sequence and relationship of events.

2.0: History Skills: Students will use social studies vocabulary and concepts to engage in inquiry, in research, in analysis, and in decision making.

3.0: Prehistory to 400 CE: Students understand the development of human societies, civilizations, and empires through 400 CE.

4.0: 1 CE to 1400: Students understand the characteristics, ideas, and significance of civilizations and religions from 1 CE to 1400.

5.0: 1200 to 1750: Students understand the impact of the interaction of peoples, cultures, and ideas from 1200 to 1750.

6.0: 1700 to 1865: Students understand the people, events, ideas, and conflicts that led to the creation of new nations and distinctive cultures.

7.0: 1860 to 1920: Students understand the importance and impact of political, economic, and social ideas.

8.0: The Twentieth Century, a Changing World: 1920 to 1945: Students understand the importance and effect of political, economic, technological, and social changes in the world from 1920 to 1945.

9.0: The Twentieth Century, a Changing World: 1945 to 1990: Students understand the shift of international relationships and power as well as the significant developments in American culture.

10.0: New Challenges, 1990 to the Present: Students understand the political, economic, social, and technological issues challenging the world as it approaches and enters the new millennium.